The First Book of

Paradox® for Windows®

The First Book of
Paradox®
for Windows®

Jonathan Kamin

alpha
books

A Division of Prentice Hall Computer Publishing
11711 North College, Carmel, Indiana 46032 USA

To Dr. Samuel G. Benson

© 1993 by Alpha Books

International Standard Book Number: 0-672-27402-7

Library of Congress Catalog Card Number: 92-82785

95 94 93   9 8 7 6 5 4 3 2 1

Interpretation of the printing code: the rightmost number of the first
series of numbers is the year of the book's printing; the rightmost
number of the second series of numbers is the number of the book's
printing. For example, a printing code of 93-1 shows that the first
printing of the book occurred in 1993.

Screen reproductions in this book were created by means of the
program Collage Plus from Inner Media, Inc., Hollis, NH.

Printed in the United States of America

Publisher
Marie Butler-Knight

Associate Publisher
Lisa A. Bucki

Managing Editor
Elizabeth Keaffaber

Acquisitions Manager
Stephen R. Poland

Production Editor
Lisa C. Hoffman

Manuscript Editors
Audra Gable,
San Dee Phillips,
Barry Childs-Helton

Cover Designer
Susan Kniola

Designer
Amy Peppler-Adams

Indexer
Jeanne Clark

Production Team
Tim Cox, Mark Enochs,
Joelynn Gifford, Tim Groeling,
Debbie Hanna, Phil Kitchel,
Tom Loveman, David
McKenna, Michael J. Nolan,
Barry Pruett, Joe Ramon,
Carrie Roth, Dennis Sheehan,
Ann Taylor, Jeff Valler, Kelli
Widdifield, Corinne Walls,
Mary Beth Wakefield

Special thanks to Hilary J. Adams for assuring the technical accuracy of this book.

Contents

9 Queries to Create New Values and Change Data   213

Introduction

Simplify, simplify.

 —Henry David Thoreau

How wonderful that we have met with Paradox. Now we have some hope of making progress.

 —Niels Bohr

Paradox for Windows is a powerful tool for managing information. Indeed, it is one of the most powerful record-management systems available for the PC and PS/2 families of computers. Normally, such power carries a price tag: harnessing it requires learning myriad commands—perhaps even a programming language. But the paradox of Paradox is its ease of use. Using simple menu commands, you can set up sophisticated data-management systems with no programming whatsoever.

The First Book of Paradox for Windows is your first step toward harnessing the power of Paradox for Windows. It guides you step-by-step from the most basic through many of the more advanced features. Quick Steps take you through the common procedures you'll use every day. Each chapter builds on the information in previous chapters, so that by the end of this book, you'll be quite comfortable with all of Paradox's main features. You'll be creating data tables and using sophisticated presentation tools with ease.

You don't need to know anything about data management to use this book. Chapter 1 explains the most basic principles, and others are introduced as needed. All you need is a basic knowledge of your computer and a willingness to learn.

How to Use This Book

The best way to use this book is to be seated at your computer with Paradox for Windows running. Then you can try out each new technique as it's introduced and gain proficiency as you read. If you're new to database management, begin with Chapter 1, "What Is Paradox for Windows?," to learn what database management software is, what it can and cannot do, and what Paradox, in particular, can do for you.

If you have experience with database management but have never used Paradox, begin with Chapter 2, "Getting Started." You'll learn about Paradox's menus and how to use them. Paradox's screen layout is described so you'll know where to look for various types of useful information. You'll learn how to get help and how to get into and out of Paradox. You'll also learn how to move through Paradox windows and menus, and how to use the mouse and the keyboard in Paradox.

Chapter 3, "Your First Table," guides you through the creation of database tables and introduces the various categories of data that Paradox can handle. In the process, you'll set up a simple database application and lay the groundwork for a more complex one to be developed later in the book.

In Chapter 4, you begin "Entering and Editing Data." You'll learn how to enter data and many ways to alter the data you have already entered. By the time you finish, you'll have an almost-usable address and phone number file.

There's no point in storing information you can't find. Sorting your data makes it easier to find what you're looking for. In addition, database management programs such as Paradox have built-in safeguards that help ensure that your data is valid. You'll learn how to use the features that accomplish these ends in Chapter 5, "Sorting and Key Fields."

Designing a data-management system is a complex task. Virtually everyone makes some design decisions they later regret. Paradox makes it easy to redesign your system. You'll learn how in Chapter 6, "Modifying and Fine-Tuning Tables." You'll also learn how to exercise precise control over the items of data that appear in your system.

With Paradox for Windows you can add memos of almost unlimited length to a database. You can also place graphic files created with other applications in a database. You'll learn how to enter and edit memos, and place graphics in both tables and forms in Chapter 7, "Working with Embedded Objects."

The reason for setting up a data-management system is to be able to get information from the data you have stored in it. Chapters 8 and 9 introduce you to the many ways of using your data to answer questions. You'll learn how to find specific items and groups of items with something in common. You'll find out how to create new values from the data you have gathered and to use these new values to change the data you have stored.

The strength of a high-level database-management system such as Paradox is its ability to deal with bodies of data that involve complex interrelationships. Paradox makes it especially easy to do so. In Chapter 10, "Creating Relationships Between Tables," you'll look at the beginnings of an order entry application that uses such complex relationships. In the process, you'll learn the basic principles of organizing data in multiple tables.

Chapter 11, "Creating and Using Design Documents," uses the tables described in Chapter 10 as the basis for new methods of presenting your data for review and consideration: forms (documents for displaying on the screen) and reports (documents to be printed). In this chapter, you'll learn many features of the document design window. Chapter 12 takes you through the Steps for "Creating Graphs."

If you do not have Paradox already running on your computer, the Appendix will tell you how to install it.

When you have finished with *The First Book of Paradox for Windows,* you'll have a basic mastery of all the major components of Paradox. You can continue to develop your skills with the help of the menus and the help screens, or you can seek further guidance from more advanced books.

Conventions Used in This Book

As you use this book, you will notice that it includes several special elements to highlight important information.

- Actions that you take, whether it's pressing a key, selecting a menu, or choosing an option, will appear in color.

- Text that you should type in is printed in `bold color computer font like this`.

- Keys that you press are shown as keycaps, such as `↵Enter` and `Tab⇄`.

- Many commands are activated by pressing two or more keys at the same time. These key presses or selections are separated by a plus sign (+) in the text. For example, "press `Alt`+`F1`" means that you should hold down the `Alt` key while you press `F1` and then release both at once (you don't type the plus sign).

- As a keyboard shortcut, commands often have a selection letter which appears underlined on-screen. In this book, the selection letter is printed in boldface for easy recognition (for example, **T**able).

- Many Paradox commands display menus of subcommands. Instructions to enter a subcommand will generally list all the commands to enter, like this: File New Form. When you see a command such as this, you press `F`, `N`, `F` in succession.

- DOS file names and commands (including the names of files you create in Paradox) are shown in all capital letters.

- Paradox operators appear in italics, for example, *changeto*.

QUICK STEPS

Look for this icon for Quick Steps that tell you how to perform important tasks in Paradox for Windows. Quick Steps and the page numbers on which they appear are listed on the inside front cover of this book.

Practical ideas for using Paradox for Windows are outlined throughout this book.

TIP: Helpful tips and shortcuts are included in Tip boxes throughout this book.

NOTE: Important information that should be noted when using Paradox for Windows is included throughout this book.

These notes warn you of potential pitfalls and problems which you should avoid when using Paradox for Windows.

Acknowledgments

No book is ever the work of a single individual, no matter what the title page says. It would have been completely impossible for me to complete the first edition of this book without the advice and guidance of Celeste Robinson. Celeste helped me conceptualize many issues, drew my attention to the essentials, and was always patient with my numerous questions.

Although my familiarity with Paradox had increased considerably before I completed the current edition, Celeste's contributions were no less essential. Martin Waterhouse and Enrique LaRoche gave me some general pointers on database design. Nan Borreson and Karen Giles of Borland International kept me abreast of developments in Paradox and kindly supplied the software. Kevin A. Smith and Quinn Wildman, also of Borland, helped clarify many obscure technical points. Not least, Lisa Bucki, of Alpha Books, gave me constant advice and support, helped determine many aspects of the book's form, and carefully developed the text. Thanks also to Lise Hoffman, Audra Gable, and San Dee Phillips of Alpha Books.

The manuscript was created with WordStar for DOS, release 7.0. Screens were captured using Inner Media's Collage Plus and refined with PC Paintbrush IV Plus. Other illustrations were prepared using Micrografx's Windows Draw!.

Trademarks

All terms mentioned in this book that are known to be trademarks or service marks are listed below. In addition, terms suspected of being trademarks or service marks have been appropriately capitalized. Alpha Books cannot attest to the accuracy of this information. Use of a term in this book should not be regarded as affecting the validity of any trademark or service mark.

Collage Plus is a trademark of Inner Media, Inc.

Microsoft Windows is a registered trademark of Microsoft Corporation.

MS-DOS is a registered trademark of Microsoft Corporation.

Object PAL is a trademark of Borland International.

OS/2 is a trademark of Microsoft Corporation.

Paradox and Quattro are registered trademarks of Borland International.

PC Paintbrush IV Plus is a trademark of ZSoft Corporation.

PS/2 is a registered trademark of International Business Machines Corporation.

Rolodex is a trademark of Rolodex Corporation.

Windows Draw! is a trademark of Micrografx.

WordStar is a registered trademark of WordStar International.

Advantages of Database Software over Paper Records

- Database software can find specific items more quickly than you can in a paper record.
- Database software can rearrange your data to give you a different view of it.
- Information in an electronic database can always be kept up-to-date.
- Database software can perform calculations based on your data to give you new information.

Elements of Database Structure

- *Field definitions* specify the amount and kind of data to be placed in each field.
- *Field names* describe the kind of data contained in the field.
- Each *record* contains information about a single object.
- *Validity checks* determine how the data should be entered and ensure that the data conforms to specifications.

Considerations in Planning a Database

- Use existing forms and reports as a basis for determining what data you need.
- Anticipate ways in which the data will be put to use.
- Name your fields logically.
- Limit the number of fields in a table. If the number of fields is getting large, you probably need several linked tables.
- Match the size of your fields to the quantity of data they can be expected to hold.

What Is Paradox for Windows?

Paradox for Windows is a *relational database-management* program. If you're new to the world of database-management software, that sentence probably doesn't mean a thing to you right now. In this chapter, however, you'll learn about databases and some fundamental terms and concepts. You'll see what makes Paradox special in the world of database-management software and what it can do for you.

If you've just obtained a copy of Paradox for Windows and you're anxious to have the program up and running, you may be tempted to skip this chapter. I urge you not to. (All right. If you must, go on to the Appendix and install the program. But after you're through, come back and read this chapter.) Although Paradox is a relatively easy program to learn and use, you will be better prepared if you understand what it's designed to do and how it does it.

What Is a Database?

A *database* is a collection of systematically organized information. You probably use databases every day, without thinking of them as such. For example, your telephone directory is a database, as is your Rolodex. A mail-order catalog may be thought of as a database. The card catalog in the library is a particularly complex database—so complicated that many public libraries have installed database-management software to handle it. (Indeed, you might even think of the library itself as a database.)

The key factor is that the information in a database is *organized*. A pile of business cards containing the same information that you keep in your Rolodex is not a database, because it's not structured. Your personal library is probably not a database for the same reason.

Why Use Database Software?

Since you already use databases every day and they work perfectly well on paper, you may wonder what advantage you'd gain by using database software on a computer. Depending on the data you want to manage, database software may not help you at all. After all, the telephone directory, for example, is a reasonably accurate guide to addresses and telephone numbers.

However, the telephone directory is updated only once a year, and it's organized in only one way: the alphabetical order of the last names of telephone-service subscribers. If you maintain extensive telephone contacts in your business, you'll want your personal phone directory to be up-to-the-minute. ("But that's what my Rolodex is for," you may protest. True enough, but read on.)

What do you do if you remember someone's first name, but not their last name? Or if you've filed an entry by the name of your contact person, and you remember only the name of the company he or she works for?

Here's where database software can really help you. Database software can arrange your information so that you can get to any item quickly and easily. If you set up your database correctly, it's equally easy to find somebody's first name, company affiliation, or last name.

Moreover, database software can provide you with many perspectives on your data that would be difficult to get when you manage your records by hand. Suppose, for example, you wanted to find out whether there is a relationship between your customers' addresses and the merchandise they ordered, or simply wanted to create a bulk-mailing list to take advantage of reduced postal rates.

If all the data were on index cards and you had many customers, it might take you several days to get the information you wanted. With database software, however, you can sort your information by Zip code, to produce the information almost instantly. Good database software can even provide you with a detailed and good-looking report summarizing the information in many different ways.

In addition, with a little effort, the information in your database can always be up-to-date. Database software allows you to add new information to a database, delete outdated information, and make other changes needed to keep your information current.

In sum, some of the biggest advantages of database software are:

- It can find any information contained in your database quickly and easily.

- It can provide you with many different views of your information.

- It allows you to maintain the information so that it's always current.

In addition, most database software also allows you to perform mathematical calculations on the stored information and to view the results.

The Parts of a Database

Although you may think otherwise, computers aren't very smart. (If they were, they'd be able to figure out what you mean when you type a command the wrong way, and they would do what you want in spite of the error.) Therefore, you have to be very careful about the information you give them and the questions you want them to answer. However, computers *are* very fast and very precise. Given properly arranged information, they can perform complex and tedious tasks (such as sorting all your alphabetized customer addresses by Zip code) quite quickly and easily.

For this reason, databases must conform to a very strict structure. They are generally set up in tables of rows and columns. All the items in a given row have something in common, and all the items in a given column have something in common. Each column represents a different *category* of data. Each row represents a single object about which you have information. For example, if you were to turn your Rolodex into a database, you might want separate columns for Names, Addresses, and Phone numbers. As a result, each row would represent a separate card.

In database lingo, these columns are called *fields,* and the rows are called *records*. Fields represent categories of information about the items in the database, and records represent the items to which the information pertains. Collectively, the set of matched records sharing the same fields makes up a *table* or a *file*. Sometimes a table is referred to as a *relation,* because it relates the categories of data (the fields) to the real-world items represented by the records. (This is where the term *relational* database comes from; it will be discussed later in the chapter.)

One important feature of databases is that fields have *field names* and records have *record numbers*. If you look at Figure 1.1, it's easy to see that each entry in the phone directory represents a record, having fields for last names, first names, addresses, cities, and phone numbers. (Some of the fields may be empty in some records.) Figure 1.2 shows an example of similar information in a Paradox for Windows database table.

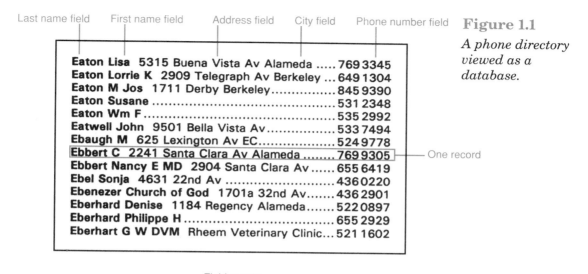

Last name field   First name field   Address field   City field   Phone number field

Figure 1.1
A phone directory viewed as a database.

One record

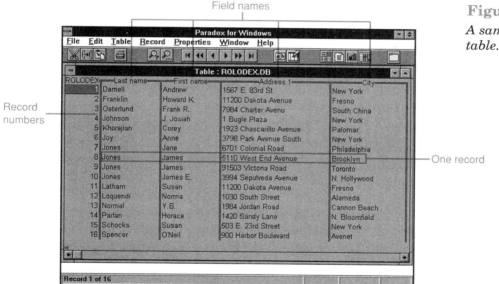

Field names

Figure 1.2
A sample Paradox table.

Record numbers

One record

To take a different example, a library card catalog always includes at least the following fields:

- Author's last name
- Author's first name
- Book title

- Publisher

- Place of publication

- Publication date

- Subject

- Library of Congress catalog number

Many libraries include even further information, such as cross-references, alternative subject headings, author's dates of birth and death, and so on. This is quite a complex database.

The field names, along with some other information, make up what is called the *structure* of a database. In addition to the names of the fields (which tell you what kind of information appears in each field), the structure also contains:

- Information about *how much* data can be stored in each field (generally expressed as a number of characters).

- Information about the *kind* of information represented by each field: text, numbers, dates, currency, and so on.

Additionally, the structure may include information about how the data is to be entered into each field (for example, whether the first character should be capitalized, and whether punctuation marks are allowed).

These examples again suggest one of the great advantages of a computerized database over a paper database. The public library generally has three card catalogs—one each for titles, authors, and subjects. In a computerized card catalog, the information for each book is recorded only once. You can use the database software to select information by title, author, or subject from the same set of records.

What Is Database Management?

Anytime you use your database software to rearrange the information in your database to get a new viewpoint, you are *managing* your database. You are also managing your database when you add information to it, change the information in it, or rearrange its organization (which is *not* the same as rearranging or editing the information).

Most importantly, you are managing your database when you extract useful information from it. In addition to browsing through a table record by record, or searching a table for specific values, there are two other ways to get information from your database.

First, you can construct a *query,* asking Paradox to show you all the records that have certain characteristics in which you're interested. Second, you can print a *report,* showing either all the information in a table, all the information in selected fields, or only the information generated by a query.

In addition, while querying or producing a report, you can ask Paradox to *calculate* values based on any numeric quantities that appear in your database. You can even save the calculated results to use again later.

In summary, database management includes the following functions:

- *Adding* information to the database.

- *Editing* the data in the database, that is, making changes to the information in specific fields and records.

- *Deleting* information from the database.

- *Searching* for various items of information in the database.

- *Sorting* the information into a usable order.

- *Querying* the database to get answers to questions about the relationships between items in your database.

- *Reporting* on the data in your database, and the relationships it represents.

- *Calculating* values based on numeric quantities.

What Is a Relational Database?

You already know that a database is a table, or relation, consisting of rows called records and of columns called fields. So what's a relational database? Basically, a relational database is a *collection* of interconnected tables—tables with *relationships* between them. Paradox, as a relational database manager, allows you to:

- Store information about the same items in several tables, and link the tables together meaningfully.

- Ask questions, or construct *queries*, about several tables at once.

- Create and manage *one-to-many* relationships, such as all the books by a given author, or all the orders taken by a given salesperson. It can manage even more complex *many-to-many* relationships, an issue I won't deal with in this book.

Because the relationships between the tables in a relational database are carefully defined (and controlled by the software), the software can do a great deal to maintain the *integrity* of your data. That is, it can discover whether the data in a table is properly linked to that in another table, and delete entries that are not so linked, or warn you so that you can make the necessary corrections.

Paradox is especially friendly in this regard. It always gives you several chances to make corrections. In addition, when you perform complex operations that may change the structure of your data, Paradox generally creates a separate table to preserve the original form of any data that you alter or delete. Thus, you can correct it and add it back into the original table if you wish.

The Importance of Planning

Paradox is called Paradox because it allows you to deal with complicated data-management problems using simple means.

Where other relational database managers require extensive programming to get answers to complex questions, you can generally get similar answers from Paradox just by filling out forms selected from menus.

If your database doesn't permit you to answer the questions you want to ask, Paradox makes it relatively easy to restructure your tables to do so. However, "relatively easy" is not the same as "a breeze." Therefore, it's important to think about the kinds of questions you might want to ask before you set up your tables. The more accurately you anticipate what information you will need, the less trouble you will have later on. Even so, no one can anticipate all possible future uses of their data.

Organizing and Defining Fields

Consider the Rolodex example. Suppose you created the following fields:

- Name

- Address

- Phone number

These are, after all, the categories in which you think of the information in your paper Rolodex. But remember, computers aren't smart—they can't anticipate the way you think.

Consider the Name field. Will you enter the names last name first, such as:

Jones, Henry

or first name first, such as:

Henry Jones

or will you leave it up to the person entering the data?

Now consider what happens when you try to sort the names in your database. Suppose the database contained the following entries:

```
Diane Smith
Fred
```

```
J. Josiah Johnson
Jones, Henry
Susan Schocks
```

If you asked your database-management software to sort these names, they would *always* come out in that order. Paradox (and virtually any other database program) will sort the data in a field character by character, starting from the left.

It doesn't understand the difference between a first name and a last name—something that's intuitive to you—unless you tell it there's a difference. So instead of a single Name field, you'd be better off with two, or possibly three, Name fields:

- Last name

- First name

- Middle initial

With separate Last and First name fields, you can ask Paradox to search for Diane Smith by looking for Diane in the First name field, or for Smith in the Last name field.

Now, what about that Middle initial field? If you use it, J. Josiah Johnson will have to become J. J. Johnson, unless you want to put Josiah in the First name field. So do you include middle initials in the First name field or not?

Basically, it depends on what you want to do with the data. Paradox is smart enough to find Josiah when one field of a record contains the data—for example, when the First name field contains:

```
J. Josiah
```

but you have to know how to ask for it. (Don't worry, you'll learn. It's not hard.)

You'll run into similar problems with the Address field. An address normally contains several distinct items, each of which might be in a separate field:

- Street address
- Apartment (or Suite number)
- City
- State
- Zip code

If you remembered the state that a person lives in (but not the city), it would be a lot easier to find the address you're looking for if these items were treated separately. And you couldn't possibly sort by Zip code for mass mailing unless the Zip code was in a separate field.

Linking Tables

Suppose you wanted to create a database containing information about a collection of record albums. If you were using a *flat-file database manager*, you would be able to handle only one table at a time. This means you would have to have a separate record for each song on each album—creating a rather unwieldy and large file.

If, however, you could *link* several tables, you could have a table containing a single entry for each album, and a second table listing the songs on all the albums, linked to the names of the albums in the first table. This is possible only with a relational database manager, such as Paradox.

This approach has many advantages:

- You don't have to type all of the information about each album over and over for each song on the album. In addition to reducing the amount of work involved, this reduces the likelihood of error.

- Proper linking of the two tables can make it easier to find the information you want.

- It's easier to manage the data, because you eliminate the redundancy created by multiple entries for each album.

Thus, with multiple tables, you add another dimension of complexity to your planning. But you also are able to handle much more complex data.

To illustrate how managing the data is made simpler, consider what happens if you want to get rid of an album. With a flat-file database, you have to take extra care to be sure you've deleted all the records pertaining to that album. With a relational database, you need to perform the deletion only once—at the main entry called the *master record*. Then, every song that is linked to this master record can be deleted automatically.

Planning Guidelines

In the course of this book, you'll see how to develop an order-entry application requiring multiple tables. However, you'll start simple, with a single, flat-file database; then you'll gradually work up to multiple tables.

By the time you deal with multiple tables, you'll have already mastered the fundamentals, and it will be relatively easy. In the meantime, keep these principles in mind:

- If you're creating a computerized version of information that's already on paper, use the paper forms and reports as the starting point for planning the structure of your database.

- Carefully consider how you will use your database. Try to anticipate future as well as present uses. This can help to ensure that you include all the fields you will need in the future as well as in the present.

- Give your field names a logical relationship to the data you expect them to hold. The more clearly you envision your data's structure, the more likely you'll be to create categories that support your search for meaningful information. For example, you might treat a person's name as two fields (First and Last) and an address as five or more fields (Company, Department, Street address, Suite, City, State, and Zip code).

- If you find yourself considering tables with a huge number of fields, you probably need several additional linked tables. Keep the structure of your tables manageable. The smaller your chunks of information, the easier they will be to work with. And ideally, a single table contains information about only one type of object—for example, a customer, an order, or a product.

- Your fields should be large enough to hold the data you want to put into them. On the other hand, if they are too large, they waste your computer's resources.

Under the best of circumstances, designing a database is a repetitive process. It's virtually inevitable that as you use your database, you'll come across variations in the data that you didn't plan for. You may have to change the structure of a field, a table, or even an entire series of linked tables.

Paradox is flexible enough to let you add fields to a table, break tables up into a series of related tables, and change the size of your fields—all without losing any data. However, the less reorganizing you have to do, the happier you'll be with the results—and the fewer headaches you'll have in the future.

Viewing and Presenting Paradox Data

If all you could do with a database-management program was enter and rearrange data, it wouldn't be very useful. Therefore, Paradox for Windows gives you many ways of viewing and presenting your data.

Forms

In addition to the standard database table, you can view or enter data in a *form*. Figure 1.3 shows an example of the standard form

Paradox creates for you, but you can create customized forms including (and excluding) whatever elements may help to make your data more comprehensible.

Figure 1.3

*A standard
Paradox form.*

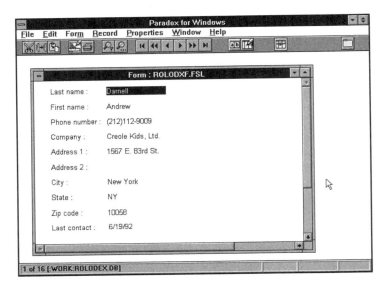

Other Types of Paradox Documents

In Paradox for Windows, forms and other means of viewing and presenting data are called *documents*.

The other type of document you can create is a *report*, which is used primarily for printing data. In addition, Paradox for Windows lets you create *graphs* as part of a form or report, and *crosstabs* (summary tables resembling spreadsheets) within a form.

Figure 1.4 shows a sample report, and Figure 1.5 shows a sample graph, along with some of the data on which it was based.

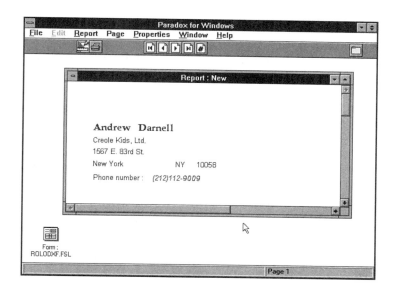

Figure 1.4
A sample report.

Graph

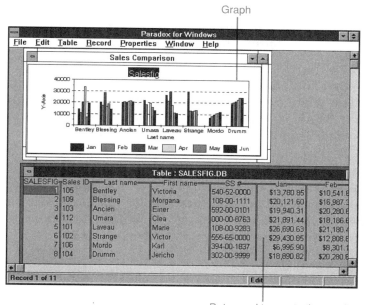

Figure 1.5
A sample graph.

Data used to create the graph

Although the illustrated form and report are rudimentary, you can change every element of the appearance of a Paradox document. You can use all the facilities of Microsoft Windows to control the size and style of type used, add text of your own, add graphic elements, and lay out the items as you see fit. You can even add new fields calculated from the values in existing fields. You can thus make your documents closely match the paper documents used by your organization, or tailor them to any purpose.

Paradox contains one more presentation tool: a *crosstab*. This is a special type of summary table which categorizes the values in one or more fields according to the values in another.

The Parts of Paradox

When you first start Paradox, you see a title screen. Shortly thereafter, you'll see the main screen shown in Figure 1.6. (You'll learn how to start Paradox in Chapter 2.) Paradox uses the metaphor of a *desktop*, on which your work appears in various *windows*.

At the top of the window is the main menu. The commands on this menu change to suit your current activity. Below it is the *speedbar*. The icons (pictures you click on) on the speedbar provide shortcuts to frequently used commands. When the desktop is empty, for example, the icons at the left of the speedbar provide quick ways of opening a table, a form, a query, a report, a script (program), and a library. The other icons allow you to group Paradox objects in folders. When you bring a file to the desktop, the icons on the speedbar change to reflect the actions you can perform in the type of window you have selected.

When you select a command from the main menu, a brief explanation of its function appears on the status line at the bottom of the screen.

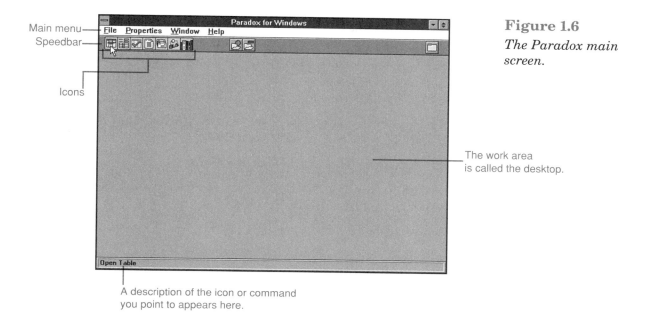

Figure 1.6
The Paradox main screen.

The Main Menu

It may not be immediately clear what each of the commands does. Don't worry about that for now. You'll learn what commands to use and when to use them in the course of this book.

Just think for a moment about what you've already learned. Using Paradox, you can create several types of *objects*: tables, forms, reports, mailmerge documents, crosstabs, and graphs.

There's also another type of object I haven't discussed yet—*scripts*. Paradox for Windows includes a powerful programming language called *ObjectPAL* (Object-oriented Paradox Application Language). You can use PAL to create extremely complex and efficient scripts—even complete applications. However, since you can do so much in Paradox without programming, we won't be dealing with scripts in this book.

The Power of Paradox

Now that you have some idea of what Paradox is, you may be interested in how much data it can handle. You'll be surprised and pleased to know the answers:

- The number of tables you can create is limited only by the capacity of your computer's hard disk.

- You can use up to 24 tables at one time.

- Each table can have up to 2 billion records, containing a total of up to 262 million characters.

- Each record can have up to 255 fields.

- Each field can have up to 255 characters.

- Any table can have a *Memo field*. The information in this field is actually stored in a separate file. The part of the Memo field that's actually in your database table can be up to 240 characters, but the entire field (including the external file) can be as large as your hard disk can handle.

- You can create an unlimited number of forms and reports for each table.

- Each form can have unlimited pages.

- You can create forms that automatically link up to five different tables, so you can enter data into as many as five different tables at once.

- When you include several tables in a single form, you can browse through the data in each of the tables while using the form.

- There is no limit to the number of pages a report may contain.

- Reports can display information from up to five tables at once.

- Any table can have a graphic field. While Paradox cannot create graphics, it can understand a wide variety of graphic file formats.

Program Requirements

To use Paradox, you must have an IBM-compatible computer with an 80286 or higher microprocessor, and at least 4MB of memory. You must have a hard disk; 12MB of hard disk space is required just to install Paradox for Windows. You must have an EGA, VGA, or higher-resolution monitor. In theory, a mouse is optional; however, you must have one to access some features. Paradox for Windows is generally much easier to use if you have a mouse.

Since Paradox for Windows is a Windows program, you must also have Microsoft Windows, version 3.0 or later, installed on your computer. To use Paradox, you must run Windows in Standard or Enhanced mode. Paradox is compatible with any network that is compatible with Microsoft Windows.

Introduction to Windows

Windows is a *graphical user interface* that runs with DOS, and adds several important features to it. The main reason many people like to work with Windows is that it presents a consistent way of interacting with the user. Virtually all of the programs that run under Windows use pull-down menus, from which you can choose commands either with the mouse or with keyboard shortcuts. When you need to give Windows (or Windows programs) more information, you are presented with a dialog box in which you either enter text in a field or select from a number of options by "pushing buttons."

Files are generally represented by icons when they are not in use, and data is displayed in framed areas called *windows*. You change your focus on the data by moving the data in the window using either a mouse or special command keys.

In addition, unlike DOS, Windows lets you run several programs at once. Windows also makes it relatively easy to transfer information from one application program to another.

Figure 1.7 shows the *Windows Program Manager,* the starting point for all your activities in Windows. You can see the special window containing the Paradox for Windows program, along with several other windows.

Figure 1.7
*The Windows
Program Manager.*

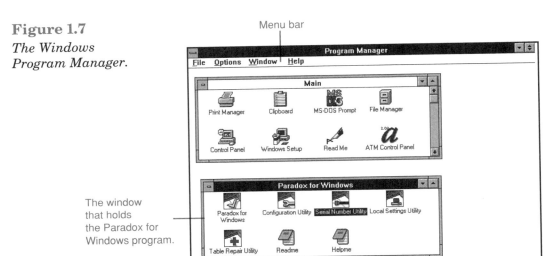

The window
that holds
the Paradox for
Windows program.

If you don't already have Windows installed, you must install it before you can use Paradox for Windows. Consult your Windows documentation for details.

If you need more information on using Windows, either *The 10 Minute Guide to Windows 3* or *The First Book of Windows 3* (or later versions of those books) can help you get started. You will be able to apply everything you learn about using Windows to your work in Paradox.

Start Paradox

1. Open the Paradox for Windows program group window.
2. Double-click on the Paradox for Windows program icon.

Choose Commands from a Menu with the Keyboard

1. Hold down Alt and the underlined letter of the command on the menu bar.
2. Press the underlined letter of the desired command.

Choose Commands from a Menu with a Mouse

1. Click on the desired command on the menu bar.
2. Click on the desired command.

Choose a Working Directory

1. Choose **F**ile **W**orking Directory.
2. Select the directory from the Database Aliases list box, if it has one, or enter its complete path name in the Path box.
3. Choose OK.

Leave Paradox

1. Choose **F**ile **E**xit.
2. Select **Y**es to save changes, and enter a name for the new file.

Getting
Started

In this chapter, you'll start up the program and learn how to use the menus and dialog boxes, the mouse, and the speedbar. You'll find out about the special keys you'll use regularly in Paradox, how to get help, and how to leave the program. As noted in Chapter 1, a mouse isn't absolutely necessary, but there are some features you can't use without one. Many others are more easily accessible if you have one.

Starting Paradox

If Paradox for Windows is not already installed on your computer, see the Appendix for instructions for doing so. Before you can install Paradox, you must install Windows. You should familiarize yourself with Windows by running the tutorial program before you attempt to use Paradox.

Starting Paradox for Windows from a DOS Prompt

You do not need to start Windows to run Paradox for Windows. If Windows is not already running and you have placed Paradox's directory on the search path (see the Appendix for details), you can start the program by typing `PDOXWIN` at the DOS prompt and pressing ⏎Enter. Paradox will load Windows for you so it can run. If the PDOXWIN directory is not on the search path, you can still run Paradox immediately by typing two commands:

```
CD\PDOXWIN

PDOXWIN
```

(Press ⏎Enter after each command.)

The first command makes Paradox's directory current and the second invokes the program. Now you're ready to start using the program.

Starting Paradox with the Mouse

If Windows is already running, you can start Paradox as you would any Windows application. Follow these Quick Steps.

QUICK STEPS — Starting Paradox with a Mouse

1. Find the Paradox for Windows group window in the Program Manager. If it's not open, open it by pressing the left mouse button twice quickly (*double-clicking*).

   Figure 1.7 shows the Paradox for Windows application group window open in the Program Manager.

2. Locate the Paradox for Windows program icon, which looks like this:

3. Double-click on this icon.

The Paradox desktop (see Figure 1.6) opens. If you have previously used the program, it restores to the desktop any items that were on it when you last closed the program.

TIP: If you have several windows open, you can make any window the active window, bringing it to the foreground, by clicking the mouse in it.

Starting Paradox from the Keyboard

1. From the Windows Program Manager, hold down Ctrl and press F6 until the Paradox for Windows window is highlighted. If it's not open, press ↵Enter.

Figure 1.7 shows the Paradox for Windows application group window open in the Program Manager.

continues

continued

2. Using the →⏎ and ←⏎ keys, move the highlight to the Paradox for Windows program icon, which looks like this:

3. Press ⏎Enter.

The Paradox desktop (see Figure 1.6) opens. If you have previously used the program, it restores any items to the desktop that were on it when you last closed the program.

How Paradox Uses Your Mouse

As noted, you can use Paradox for Windows a lot more easily with a mouse than without. Paradox assumes you have a two-button mouse. If you have a third button, Paradox ignores it. (All references to the left and right buttons assume you have not used the Windows Setup program to set up your mouse as a left-handed mouse, in other words, reversing the left and right buttons.) Following are the basic mouse techniques:

Point | Move the mouse pointer to an item on the screen.

Click | Press and release the left mouse button to select the item on which the mouse pointer rests. In menus and on the speedbar, clicking executes the selected command. In dialog boxes, clicking on a button completes the action indicated on the button.

Double-click   Press and release the left mouse button twice quickly to open a window that has been reduced to an icon, or to start a process.

Drag   Press and hold the left mouse button while moving the mouse to move an object or change its size or shape.

Right-click   Press and release the right mouse button to view the Object Inspector, which displays a menu of commands you can use to change the appearance or behavior of the selected item. You use the Object Inspector the same way as other menus, as described later in the chapter.

The Paradox Desktop

Figure 2.1 shows the Paradox desktop with several windows open. Using this figure as a guide, you can explore these features of the desktop and its windows that are present no matter what type of window is current.

Both the desktop and each window have a *title bar*. The desktop's title bar shows the program name Paradox for Windows. A window's title bar shows you some combination of the name of the file in the window, the type of file it is, and the mode it's in. When you *create* a new file, it is given the name *New*.

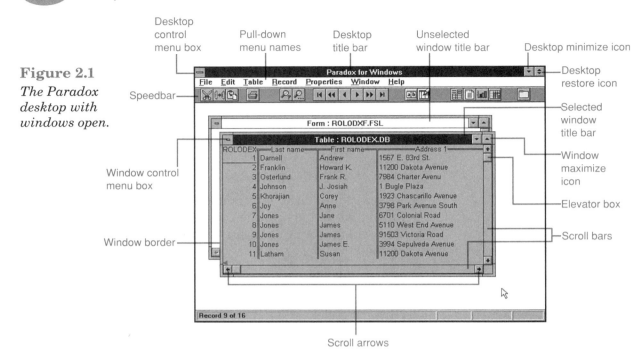

Figure 2.1
The Paradox desktop with windows open.

At the right end of the title bar are the minimize and the restore or maximize icons. If a program window does not occupy the full screen, you'll see an up-arrow (maximize icon), as you do on the Table:ROLODEX.DB title bar. Clicking this button enlarges a program window to the full size of the screen, or a file window to the full size of the desktop. When the window is at its maximum size, the arrow changes to a double arrow (restore icon), as you see on the Paradox for Windows title bar. Clicking on this arrow reduces the window to its former size. To the left of this button is another with a down-arrow. Clicking on this button *minimizes* the window, reducing it to an icon, as shown in Figure 2.2.

In the upper left corner of the screen, and of each window, is a *Control menu*. To display this menu, shown in Figure 2.2, click on the box with the bar in it, or press Alt + Spacebar. As you can see, you can control the size and shape of the window from this menu, as well as switch to other applications. The Control menu on the file windows, shown in Figure 2.3, lets you switch from one Paradox window to another, rather than from one Windows application to another.

Desktop control menu box

Desktop control menu

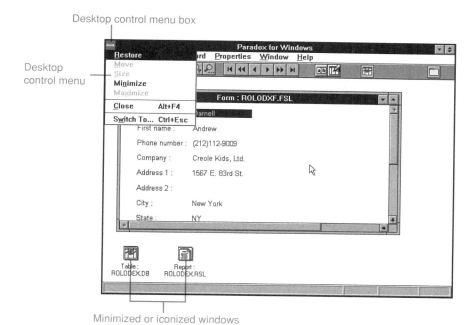

Minimized or iconized windows

Figure 2.2
The Control menu and some iconized windows.

Window control menu

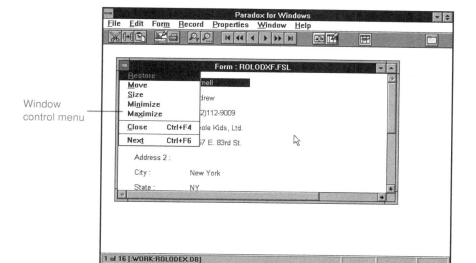

Figure 2.3
The Control menu on a Paradox window.

Below the window's title bar is the *menu bar*, containing the names of the *pull-down menus* appropriate to the window that's currently selected. Before this chapter is over, you'll learn how to pull down and use these menus.

The next item on the screen is the *speedbar*. This consists of a series of icons which let you perform various actions quickly without going through the menus. If you compare Figure 2.1 with Figure 1.6, you'll see that the items on the speedbar change depending on what's currently on the desktop. (The same is true of the pull-down menus.)

At the right side and along the bottom of each window are *scroll bars*. Click on these bars, or drag the elevator box, or click on the scroll arrows at the ends of the scroll bars to see other portions of the file in the window.

Notice that one window has a dark title bar and the others have light ones. The one with the dark title bar is *selected, active,* or *current*. The commands on the menu, and the icons on the speedbar, pertain to actions you can take in this window. To make another window current with the mouse, just click in it, and you'll see the menu and speedbar change accordingly. (A little later, you'll learn how to accomplish these tasks with the keyboard.)

Every window has a *border*. You can use the border to change a window's size. Move the mouse pointer to the border so that the pointer becomes a two-headed arrow. When it does, click and drag the border to make the window larger or smaller. If you start at a corner, you can change the size of the window both horizontally and vertically at once.

At the bottom of the screen is the *status bar*. Here you'll see an explanation of a selected command or speedbar button, or, if neither is selected, some indication of where you are in a window and what you're doing.

On the right side of the status bar are three little boxes. When you're working in a window, these boxes may display information about the current state of the object you're working on—information such as whether you can edit the data, whether you're in a mode where you can move the cursor within a field, or whether the record can be accessed by others on a network.

Using Paradox Menus

There are several ways to get around in Paradox's menus, both with the keyboard and the mouse. Look at them all now. Figure 2.4 shows the **F**ile menu, which is the same no matter which type of window is current. Refer to this figure while studying the next set of Quick Steps.

Grayed commands are currently unavailable.

Choosing a command with a pointer displays a submenu.

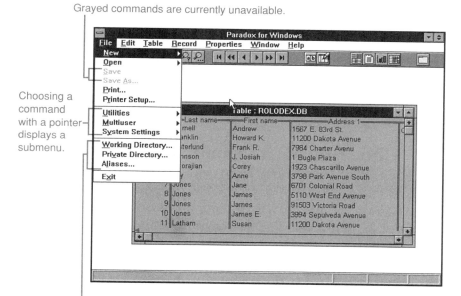

Choosing a command with an ellipsis displays a dialog box.

Figure 2.4
The File menu.

Notice that most of the commands on the menu are black, while a few are gray. The gray commands are not available at present. When they can be executed, they will become black.

Some commands have a small pointer at the right margin. Choosing one of these commands displays a submenu.

Other commands have an ellipsis. Choosing one of these commands displays a dialog box, where you will be asked for further information.

In the future, when I refer to commands on the menu, I'll tell you to *choose* a command. A command will normally include several parts. Thus, if I tell you to "choose File New Table," I mean that you should pull down the File menu, select the **New** command from that menu, and then select the **T**able command from the submenu attached to the **N**ew command.

Choosing Commands with a Mouse

If you have a mouse, you'll undoubtedly find it most convenient for choosing menu commands most of the time. The following Quick Steps show you how.

Choosing Menu Commands with the Mouse

1. Move the pointer to a command on the menu bar and click.	The menu drops down, displaying the available commands.
2. If the command you want isn't visible, click on other menu names, or drag the mouse along the menu bar to see the contents of other menus.	
3. When you find the command you want, click on it.	Paradox executes the command.

To close an open menu, press Esc, or click on the desktop outside the menu and outside of any windows. (If you click in a window, it may change what you see in that window.)

Choosing Menu Commands from the Keyboard

There are two, and sometimes three, ways to choose commands without using a mouse. Even if you have a mouse, you may find these methods convenient when you're deeply involved in entering or editing data, because you won't want to take your hands off the keyboard.

Choosing Commands with the Keyboard

1. Press [Alt].

The menu bar becomes active, with the **F**ile command highlighted.

2. Press [↵Enter] to display that menu, or the [→] and [←] keys to move to other menus.

Paradox displays the menu, or moves the highlight to another menu.

3. If you moved the highlight, press [↵Enter] when the desired menu is highlighted.

Paradox displays the menu.

4. Use the [↑] and [↓] keys to move to the command you want.

5. Press [↵Enter].

Paradox executes the command.

You may have noticed that every menu on the menu bar, and every command on the menus attached to the menu bar, has one underlined letter in its name. You can use these *selection letters* to choose commands from menus with the keyboard as well.

Choosing Commands by Selection Letter

1. Hold down Alt and press the underlined letter in the name of the menu you want.

The menu drops down.

2. Press the underlined letter in the name of the command you want.

Paradox executes the command, or displays a submenu, or displays a dialog box.

Finally, many commands have *shortcut keys*, as you can see in Figure 2.5. These keys are either function keys, combinations of a function key and one of the shift-state keys (Ctrl , ⇧Shift , and Alt)), or combinations of the Ctrl key and a letter key. As you can see in the figure, some shortcuts require three keys. (You can also see a submenu in this figure.) If you can remember these key combinations, you'll find them faster than other methods of executing commands.

Figure 2.5
A menu showing shortcut keys.

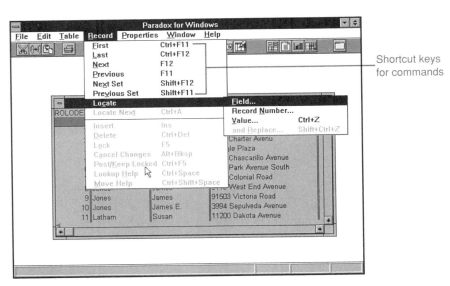

Shortcut keys for commands

Moving Among Windows

The easiest way to move among windows is to select the one you want with the mouse. However, there are several other ways. As you saw in Figure 2.3, each window's Control menu includes the command:

Next   Ctrl+F6

You can move from one window to another with this key combination just as you can in the Windows Program Manager. As with the Program Manager, this key combination takes you to each window in turn, whether the window is open or reduced to an icon.

Additionally, you can use the **W**indow menu, which appears whenever any files are open. Figure 2.6 shows the **W**indow menu. As you can see, each window that's on the desktop appears by name, with an underlined number next to it. You can choose a window by selecting it from this menu, or by pressing the key corresponding to its number.

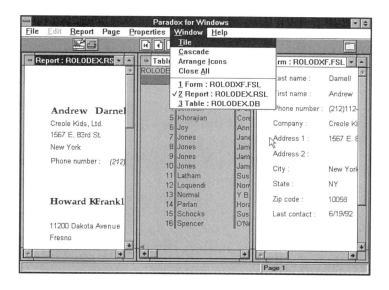

Figure 2.6

The Window menu with tiled windows.

Four other commands on the Window menu let you arrange the appearance of windows on your desktop.

Tile	Makes all open windows of equal size, and arranges them so that they fill the desktop, as shown in Figure 2.6.
Cascade	Places all open windows in a neat, overlapping stack, as shown in Figure 2.1.
Arrange **I**cons	Neatly aligns the icons representing minimized windows.
Close **A**ll	Closes all open windows, asking you first if you want to save any work you haven't yet saved.

Using Dialog Boxes

As noted, when a menu option is followed by an ellipsis, choosing it will display a dialog box. Figure 2.7 shows two Paradox dialog boxes. If you're familiar with Windows, you'll notice that their appearance is somewhat different from standard Windows dialog boxes. The various "buttons" are different shapes, and many of the options don't have underlined selection letters. You can select those that do by holding down Alt and pressing the underlined letter, just as you would in a menu.

To move from one item in a dialog box to another with a mouse, you simply move the mouse pointer to the item you want and click. With the keyboard, you move between major areas of the box, and command buttons, with the Tab and ⇧Shift+Tab keys. You can see what's selected because a dotted line appears around it, as on the Find... button. In theory, you can move from one boxed region in a dialog box to another using the F3 and F4 keys, but this doesn't work at present.

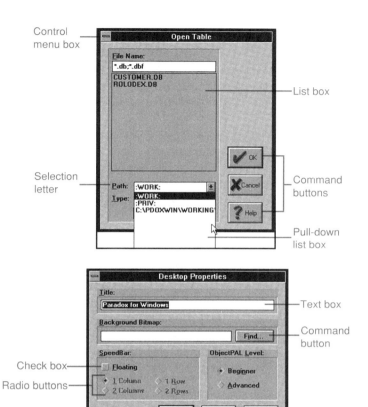

Figure 2.7
Typical Paradox dialog boxes.

Let's briefly review the functions of the elements you see here, and how to use them.

Text boxes (sometimes called edit boxes) are white rectangular areas in which you enter text, such as a filename or a field name. *List boxes* let you select items from a list. If the list is too long to fit in the box, a scroll bar appears on its right margin. To select items in a list box, use the ⬆ and ⬇ keys to move the highlight to the item you want, then press ⏎Enter.

Pull-down list boxes display only one selection until they are selected. You display the items in the list by clicking on the arrow button or by pressing Alt+⬇. Select items the same way as you would in regular list boxes.

Radio buttons are small diamonds that you use to choose one of several options. You move among them with the ⬆ and ⬇ keys. When you've made your selection, press Tab⤒ to move to another part of the dialog box.

Check boxes toggle options on and off. Click in the box or press Spacebar to check an unchecked box, or remove the check from a box.

Command buttons may bring up other dialog boxes (if the command has an ellipsis), or commit you to some action. Almost every dialog box has command buttons for Help, Cancel, and OK. The Cancel button closes the dialog box without changing anything, while the OK button sets the options or carries out the commands you have selected. To use a command button, click on it, or press ↵Enter when it's selected.

If you want to back out of a dialog box, you can do so by pressing Esc or by double-clicking the Control menu box at the upperleft corner, as well as by choosing Cancel.

Special Keys in Paradox

In addition to its many shortcut keys, Paradox for Windows has many special keys and key combinations which provide the only means of accomplishing some tasks. Some are specific to a particular activity. You'll learn about those when you learn the activity to which they are appropriate. Table 2.1 is a list of special keys that are effective throughout Paradox, or in most types of windows.

Table 2.1
Paradox Special Keys

Key	Function
F1	Opens the Help system, displaying helpful information appropriate to your current activity.
F2, Ctrl+F	Enters and leaves *Field view*, in which you can edit the contents of a field without erasing the field.
Ctrl+F2	In Field view, moves to the next field without leaving Field view.

Key	Function
`⇧Shift`+`F2`, `Ctrl`+`T`	Enters and leaves *Memo view*, which allows you to view a memo or embedded object.
`F3`	Moves to the previous form in a series of linked forms.
`⇧Shift`+`F3`	Moves back a page.
`F4`	Moves to the next form in a series of linked forms.
`⇧Shift`+`F4`	Moves forward a page.
`Alt`+`F4`	Closes the current window, asking you first if you want to save any changes. If no windows are open, closes Paradox.
`F6`	Opens the Object Inspector for the selected object.
`⇧Shift`+`F6`	If several objects are selected, opens the Object Inspector for all of them.
`Ctrl`+`F6`	Moves from one window to the next.
`F7`	Toggles between Form view (a display of your data one record at a time in a form) and Table view.
`F8`	In forms and reports toggles between View mode and Design mode.
`F9`	Toggles between View mode and Edit mode.
`F10`, `Alt`	Activates the menu bar.
`F11`	Moves to the previous record.
`F12`	Moves to the next record.
`Esc`	Closes a menu or dialog box without making any changes.
`◆Backspace`	Erases a character to the left.
`Ctrl`+`◆Backspace`	Erases the word to the left of the cursor.
`Ctrl`+`Z`	Finds a specified value.
`⇧Shift`+`Ctrl`+`Z`	Finds a specified value, replaces it with another specified value.
`Ctrl`+`A`	Finds the next instance of a specified value.

Getting Help

One very useful menu in Paradox is **Help**. Help is always available no matter what you're doing in Paradox. To get help, just press F1. If you're working in a window, Paradox will display help information on the current type of file, or your current mode of activity in that window. If you're in a dialog box, you'll see information on the selected option. You can also get help in a dialog box by clicking the Help button.

When you open the Help menu, you see the options shown in Figure 2.8. If you select Contents, you'll see a list of major topics, as shown in Figure 2.9. Click on any icon, or any text that is underlined and highlighted in green to see further information on the object or topic. You may want to begin with Essentials, which presents a more detailed list of topics.

Figure 2.8

The Help menu.

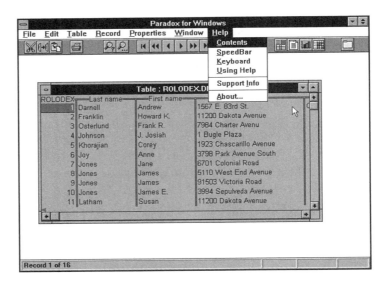

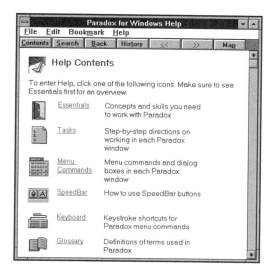

Figure 2.9
The Help system Contents.

Each Help window gives you the following additional options, either through the menus within the Help window or through the buttons below the menu:

Contents	Clicking this button or pressing `Alt`+`C` returns you to the Contents screen.
Search	Clicking this button or pressing `Alt`+`S` lets you select or type keywords to search for, and shows you a list of Help topics mentioning them.
Back	Clicking this button or pressing `Alt`+`B` takes you to the screen you viewed previously.
His**t**ory	Clicking this button or pressing `Alt`+`T` displays a list of the Help topics you have viewed since you opened the Help system, in reverse order.

>>	Clicking this button or pressing [Alt]+[>] takes you to the next related Help topic.
<<	Clicking this button or pressing [Alt]+[<] takes you to the previous related Help topic.
Ma**p**	Clicking this button or pressing [Alt]+[P] displays the graphic map of the Help system shown in Figure 2.10. Press [Alt]+[O] or click the Home button to return from the map to the Contents screen.
File **P**rint Topic	Choosing this command *within the Help window* or pressing [Alt]+[F] and then [P] prints the current screen.
Help Always on **T**op	Choosing this command *within the Help window* or pressing [Alt]+[H] and then [T] makes the Help icon appear on the Paradox desktop. This item is a toggle.

CAUTION   If you select **H**elp Always on **T**op, Windows may take you to the Help system rather than Paradox for Windows when you cycle through open applications with [Alt]+[Tab⇆], especially if you are returning from a DOS application, rather than a Windows application.

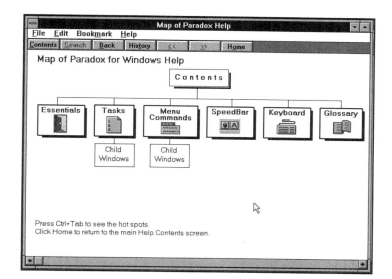

Figure 2.10
The Help map.

How Paradox Relates to Your System

Now that you've seen how to get around in Paradox for Windows, let's explore the relationship between the program and the rest of your system. Begin by taking a look at the **F**ile menu, as shown in Figure 2.11.

Special Directories

We'll be working now with the commands in the next-to-last part of the menu: **W**orking Directory, **P**rivate directory, and **A**liases. Your *working directory* is the one containing the files with which you will be working for the current session. Your *private directory* is the directory where Paradox stores all its temporary files and work files.

Figure 2.11
The File menu.

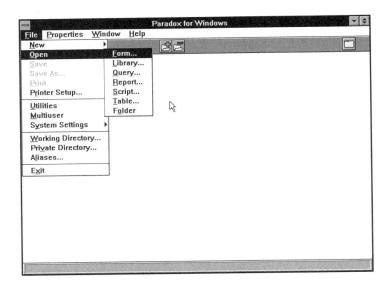

Ideally, neither of these should be the PDOXWIN directory. You don't want to put your data files among your program files because it's hard to find them. You'll want to keep the files relating to a particular project in a single directory, or a group of related directories.

It's especially important to establish a private directory if you're on a network, but it's a good idea in any case. Paradox uses a limited number of standard names for its temporary and working files. If you're on a network, and you don't select a private directory that only you have access to, other people using Paradox on the network may take actions that overwrite your working files with their own—before you're finished using the ones you created.

To designate a working directory, choose the File Working Directory command. You'll see the dialog box shown in Figure 2.12. Type in the name of your working directory and then choose OK. Don't worry about the other items in the box for now; we'll get to them soon.

Figure 2.12
The Set Working Directory dialog box.

NOTE: If you plan to follow along with the exercises in this book, open the Windows File Manager and create a new directory called LEARNPDX. When you return to Paradox, make that the working directory.

Choosing a Working Directory

1. Choose File Working Directory.

Paradox displays the Set Working Directory dialog box.

2. If you have already given the working directory an alias, as described below, pull down the Aliases list box and select the alias from your working directory from the list. If the directory you want doesn't have an alias, enter its complete path name in the Working Directory box.

3. Choose OK.

Paradox makes your chosen directory current, and thereafter looks for files only in that directory until you direct it otherwise.

To select your private directory, choose the File Private Directory command. You'll see a similar dialog box. Use the same procedure you used to select a working directory, but make sure the directory you choose is one that only *you* have access to.

Using Aliases

Paradox keeps track of your private and working directories—as well as other directories to which you may want easy access—by means of *aliases*. These are simply shortened names for directory paths.

Understanding aliases requires a slight reorientation in your thinking. Paradox wants you to think of a database as a collection of objects, rather than as a table or a file. It may consist of one or more tables, plus any number of associated forms, reports, mailmerge documents, illustrations, and other files, which you would normally keep in a single directory. Although you define an alias by giving a new name to a directory, Paradox thinks of that new name as a name for a database.

There are three reasons you'd want to use aliases. First, alias names can be selected from a drop-down list box, and are also a lot easier to type than long path names. Suppose you have an address-and-phone-number database in a directory called C:\SALES\CLIENTS\LOCAL\NEW. You could name your database (in other words, your directory) `New_Clients`, which is a lot easier to remember than the complete path name. You also have the option of selecting this database just by opening the Working Directory dialog box and selecting the alias.

Second, suppose you are working on several projects involving databases. As you switch from one to another, you'll need to change your working directory. It's a lot easier to change your working directory by selecting a project name from a list than it is to type in a path name—even if you use the File Browser (about which I'll say more shortly) to help you find the directory you want.

Third, if you become proficient enough in Paradox to program in ObjectPAL, you'll find that it's a lot easier to distribute your applications to others if they refer to databases by aliases, rather than by specific directory names.

When you installed Paradox for Windows, it created directories called PRIVATE and WORKING as subdirectories of the PDOXWIN directory. By default, these will be your private and working directories, respectively.

Let's get some hands-on experience with aliases. Choose the File Aliases command, and you'll see the Alias Manager, as shown in Figure 2.13. You'll see the alias WORK in the Database Alias text box. If you've made LEARNPDX your working directory, you should see that in the Path text box. It's there because you assigned it in the Set Working Directory dialog box. This indicates that Paradox automatically assigns the alias WORK to whatever you choose as the working directory. If you open the Database Alias list box, you should also see the reserved alias PRIV. If you select that alias, you should see the name of your private directory in the Path text box.

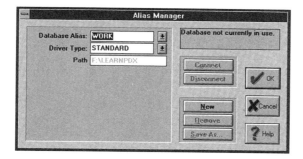

Figure 2.13
The Alias Manager.

Because Paradox assigns the alias WORK to whatever you've designated as your working directory, you should have a second alias for the LEARNPDX directory, so you can return to it after you've used another directory. Use the following Quick Steps, and enter `Examples` as the new alias for LEARNPDX. Then, if you need to use a different working directory, you can return to LEARNPDX by opening the Set Working Directory dialog box and choosing Examples from the Aliases list box. Whenever you create or change an alias, you are making it permanent. If you choose to, Paradox writes it into a file called Odapi.CFG, in the windows system directory.

Assigning a New Alias

1. Choose File Aliases.	Paradox displays the Alias Manager.
2. Press Alt + N or click the New button.	The Database Alias and Path boxes will clear.
3. Enter the new alias in the Database Alias box.	
4. Enter the complete directory path to the database in the Path box.	
5. Choose Keep New.	Paradox displays the message Alias available for this session; choose Save As to save permanently in the message area at the upper right corner of the Alias Manager.
6. Choose Save As....	A new dialog box appears, with the default filename ODAPI. and the default file specification as *.CFG.
7. If the file name ODAPI.CFG appears in the list of Existing File Names, choose it and choose OK.	Paradox displays the message File 'C:\WINDOWS\...\ODAPI.CFG' already exists. Overwrite?
8. If it does not, click Browse, and search for it. Likely locations are your WINDOWS\SYSTEM directory, your private directory, and the directory designated by the TEMP	

environment variable.
When you find it, select
it and choose OK.

9. Choose Yes.

Until you remove the alias, it will appear in the Database
Alias drop-down list box, and any other place where a list of aliases
is available. To remove an alias, follow these Quick Steps.

Removing an Alias

1. Select the alias to remove
from the Database Alias
list box.

2. Choose Remove.   Paradox displays the message `Database removed from`
`configuration file`.

Don't try to use the Alias Manager to select a   CAUTION
different working or private directory. Use the
Working Directory or Private directory commands for that
purpose. The Alias Manager only assigns a new alias to an
existing directory, not a new directory to an existing alias.

Using the Browser

Paradox includes a tool to help you find files and directories—the
Browser. The way it looks and works depends on how you get to it.
You may have noticed a **B**rowse button on several of the dialog
boxes you just used. You'll also see such a button if you use the
speedbar buttons to open a file.

There are two types of Browsers, one for directories and another for files. You'll see the directory Browser if you choose the Browse button in the dialog box that appears when you change your private directory or your working directory. You'll see such a Browser in Figure 2.14. It shows a directory tree.

If you pull down the Aliases list, you'll see a list of drive names, plus PRIV and WORK. If you select a different drive in this box, you'll see the tree change accordingly. If you select PRIV or WORK, only the directory associated with that alias and its subdirectories will appear in the tree window. (Any directory that has subdirectories is represented by a shaded folder. Double-click the shaded folder to see the subdirectories.) Once you've selected a drive, select the directory you want by clicking it. You'll see the list of files change accordingly.

Figure 2.14

A directory Browser.

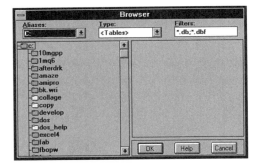

When you reach the Browser by means of a **Browse** button in a dialog box for opening a file, it looks and works a bit differently. If you select one of the File Open commands, or click on a speedbar button to open a file, you'll see a list box with a **Browse** button. Click that button and you'll see a Browser with the appropriate file type already selected and a few additional buttons, as shown in Figure 2.15. Each file of the type you selected is shown in the right window, represented by the same icon that denotes its type on the speedbar. When you see the one you want to load, double-click it, and Paradox will place its name in the text box of the dialog box containing the **Browse** button. Choose OK to bring it to the desktop.

Figure 2.15
A file Browser.

Using Folders

Sometimes you may want to use files from more than one directory. Although only one directory can be the working directory, you can give yourself ready access to files from more than one directory by using the *Folder*.

To add an item to your folder, click the Add Folder Item icon on the speedbar or choose File Open Folder. If you choose the menu command, a new **F**older menu appears on the menu bar. From that menu, choose Add Item. At this point (or when you click the Add Folder Item icon) you'll see a standard file selection dialog box. The big difference between this one and others is that you can access all the files in the current directory, not just files of one type. This difference is reflected in the Browser attached to the **B**rowse button as well.

What you see in the select file window is determined by which directory you select, and what you do with the other two boxes. Pull down the Type box, and you'll see a list of types of files, most of them associated with a specific program. By default, the box shows <Tables>, which is represented in the Filters box by *.*. When you choose a different file type, the wild-card pattern changes to match only those files you have specified (sometimes more than one wild-card pattern may appear). You can also edit the wild-card pattern to limit the files shown.

You can choose any file from this Browser and add it to your folder. You can then access it directly from the Paradox desktop by opening the folder and selecting its icon.

Each type of file is represented in the folder window by the icon that matches the type of file it is. The distinctive icons match those on the speedbar. When you see the one you want to load, double-click it, and Paradox will bring it to the desktop.

While you're dealing with the Folder, take note of the other items on the **F**older menu:

R*emove Item* deletes an item from the folder (as does the Remove Folder Item icon).

*Tidy **I**cons* arranges the icons in the folder in an orderly manner.

*Show **A**ll Files* displays all the files in the current directory in your folder, along with any you have selected.

Figure 2.16 shows a full folder.

Figure 2.16

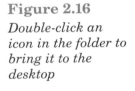

Double-click an icon in the folder to bring it to the desktop

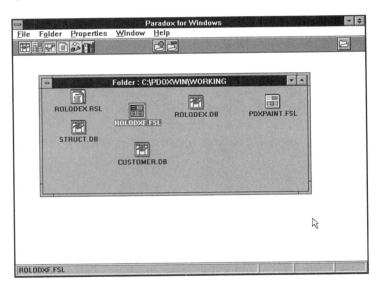

CAUTION   When you change your working directory, everything is removed from both your desktop and your folder. Use the Folder to access files on other directories *without* changing your working directory.

Leaving Paradox

There are four ways to leave Paradox for Windows:

- Use the File Exit command.
- Press Alt + F4.
- Pull down the Control menu and choose Close.
- Double-click the Control menu box (also called *close box*).

Leaving Paradox

1. Choose File Exit, press

Paradox either returns you to the Windows Program manager or if you have made changes, Paradox displays the name of the file and asks if you want to save it. If you have created new documents, Paradox displays an icon of the appropriate type and asks if you want to save the document.

2. Choose Yes to save the changes, or No to discard them. If the document is new, you'll be asked for a filename.

Paradox presents a list of current filenames and appropriate extensions.

3. To replace an existing document, select its name from the list. To give the document a new name, enter the filename without an extension and choose OK.

In This Chapter

Create a Table

1. Select File New Table and select OK.
2. For each field, enter a field name and and a data type in the appropriate columns for each field you want in the database. If the field is an Alphanumeric or Memo field, enter a field size in the Size column.
3. If the field is to be a key field, move to the Key column and double-click the left button or press Spacebar. Press Tab, ↵Enter, or →.
4. Select Save As... and give the table a name.
5. Press ↵Enter or select OK.

Search for Data

1. Select Record Locate Value.
2. Enter the value to search for and press ↵Enter or select OK.

Your First Table

Now that you know how to find your way around in Paradox, let's get to work. In this chapter, you'll create, modify, and edit a ROLODEX table. To get the most out of this book, follow the steps described to complete the table. You'll be using the table throughout most of the book to complete exercises.

The Structure of a Table

As you may remember, a database table has a strict structure. It is defined by three items:

- The *names* of its fields.

- The *size* of each field. (The number of characters each field can hold.)

- The *data type* of each field. (The kind of information it can contain.)

As you'll see shortly, fields in Paradox have one additional characteristic—whether or not they are *key fields*. Key fields control the order in which records appear, and have other important effects when you use several tables together. Ignore them for now. You'll learn about key fields in Chapter 5.

To create a table, you use the File New Table command. At this point, Paradox displays the Table Type dialog box shown in Figure 3.1. Since Paradox for Windows is the default, just select OK. You'll then see a window entitled Create Paradox for Windows Table: (Untitled), which should look like Figure 3.2.

Figure 3.1

Selecting a table type.

Figure 3.2

An empty Field Roster window.

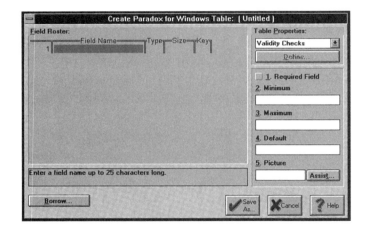

Filling Out the Field Roster

The Field Roster window gives you access to several advanced features that we won't deal with just now. Direct your attention to the left side of the window. The Field Roster is a *structure table*, not a database table. However, you fill it out the same way as you do a database table. It's set up the same way, too.

This table has five columns. As you would expect in a database table, it has field names and record numbers. The 1 in the first column is a record number. The other columns represent the fields of the database—Field Name, (Field) Type, Size, and Key. As you move from one field to the next, a prompt with an explanation appears below the table.

Field Names

At present, when the Field Name column is selected, the explanation reads:

```
Enter a field name up to 25-characters long.
```

This tells you just about everything you need to know to enter a valid field name. The field names you enter into this field will become the column headings (field names) of the table you are creating. To summarize the restrictions:

- Field names cannot be longer than 25 characters.

- No two fields can have the same name.

- Field names may contain spaces but may not begin with spaces.

- Field names may not contain the left or right bracket ([,]), left or right brace ({,}), or left or right parentheses ((,)).

- Field names may not contain a hyphen followed by a less-than symbol (->).

- Field names may not consist only of a pound sign (#).

You won't get any error messages if you violate these rules. However, you will have some trouble when you work with several tables, so follow them anyway.

CAUTION

TIP: Give fields names that accurately describe their contents. Paradox won't care what you call your fields as long as they conform to the rules.

You are now ready to enter information into the Field Name field of record number 1. Since you're creating a Rolodex file, type the field name `Last name`. Paradox will capitalize the first character for you automatically.

There are four ways to make corrections if you make typing errors:

- Press `Backspace` to delete one character at a time.
- Press `Ctrl`+`Backspace` to clear the field and start over.
- Press `F2` to switch to Field view.
- Move out of the field with the Tab, Enter, or cursor keys, and then move back to it. When you return to the field, the entire value will be highlighted. If you press any key but `F2`, the current value will be deleted and replaced by what you type.

In Field view, as you remember, you can move through and edit an entry field. When you're not in Field view, you can only clear the field and start over. Table 3.1 summarizes the keys used in Field view. Remember to press `Enter` when you are finished editing the field name.

Table 3.1
Keys Used in Field View

Key	Effect
`Backspace`	Deletes the character to the left of the cursor.
`Del`	Deletes the character at the cursor.
`Ctrl`+`Backspace`	Clears the entry field.
`←`	Moves the cursor one character to the left.
`→`	Moves the cursor one character to the right.
`Home`	Moves the cursor to the beginning of the entry field.
`Esc`	Moves the cursor to the end of the entry field.
`F2`	Ends Field view.

When you've finished entering text, press `Tab` or `Enter` to move the cursor to the next field.

Data Types and Their Sizes

Now you are in the Field Type field. Remember, a field is defined by three elements: its name, size, and data type. Your choice of a data type determines:

- How the data will appear on-screen.

- How the data may be entered.

- What kinds of operations can be performed on it.

- How much data the field can hold.

There are, however, ways you can alter the first two items to some degree. You'll look at how numeric data appears on the screen in Chapter 4. As you'll learn in Chapter 6, you can use various types of validity checks to limit the numbers entered to acceptable values. You can also improve numeric formats, just as you might in a spreadsheet.

When you enter the Field Type column, the help message at the bottom of the window tells you to:

```
Right click or press Spacebar to choose a field type.
```

Click the right mouse button or press [Spacebar] and you'll see the Type menu shown in Figure 3.3. As you can see, Paradox lets you set up fields of many types. However, for most database applications, you'll use only a few of them—alphanumeric, numeric, currency, date, and memo. The following sections provide a brief description of these data types and their characteristics.

Figure 3.3

The data type menu.

Alphanumeric Data

The alphanumeric data type can contain any combination of characters and spaces. They are used for data that will be treated as text, and will not be used in numeric operations. An A in the Type column indicates the alphanumeric data type.

Memo Data

The memo data type is an alphanumeric field of virtually unlimited length. Memo fields have two parts—a visible section that appears in the table, and a hidden section, which is stored in a separate file. You must specify the width of the visible portion of a Memo field, which can be up to 240 characters. Memo fields are indicated by an M in the Type column.

To edit a memo, or view the part of a memo that extends beyond the specified field width, press F2 to go into Field view. This brings up the Memo Editor, which works very much like the Windows Notepad.

The portion of a memo that extends beyond the visible section can be as large as 64 MB—unless you run out of disk space first. Paradox stores all the memos for a given table in a single file, separate from the table file.

Numeric Data

The numeric data type can contain any type of numeric data, with or without decimal parts. They also can contain parentheses and plus or minus signs. Use the Numeric data type for any data on which you expect to perform arithmetic operations. By default, numeric fields are formatted in the Windows number format, which you can change using the International section of the Windows Control Panel. Later you'll learn ways to assign different numeric formats to numeric fields. Numeric fields are indicated by an N in the Type column.

Do not use the Numeric data type for such items as phone numbers, Zip codes, or Social Security numbers. Data which includes punctuation as well as numbers, and which will not be used in arithmetic operations, should be treated as Alphanumeric.

CAUTION

Currency Data

The currency data type also can contain only numeric data. However, by default, numeric fields are formatted in the Windows number format, which you can change using the International section of the Windows Control Panel. Currency fields are indicated by a $ in the Type column.

Date Data

The date data type can contain only valid date values. Paradox checks all entries to make sure that the entered date is a real date. Dates must be entered in the following format:

```
[m]m/dd/[yy]yy
```

where the values shown in brackets are optional. The D's stand for the day of the month, M's for the month, and Y's for the year. (That's so you can specify one-digit days and months, and years not in the twentieth century.) By default, the date will be displayed in the short date format you selected in the Windows Control Panel International section. However, as you'll learn in Chapter 6, you can change the displayed format to one of two other styles.

Valid dates are any dates between January 1, 100 and December 31, 9999, based on the current (Gregorian) calendar. Paradox can do *date arithmetic* on data stored in Date format—that is, it can calculate a date a given number of days before or after a given date, or find the number of days between two dates.

Other Data Types

The somewhat more advanced data types for which you may have some use are:

- *Formatted Memo*, which allows you to use any of the fonts, sizes, styles, and colors of text available to you in Windows. You edit formatted memo fields the same way you do memo fields. The only difference is that you can style the text.

- *Graphic* fields, which can contain any Windows bitmap graphic image—any file with a .BMP, .TIF, .PCX, .GIF, or .EPS extension, or any graphic image you can get onto the Clipboard.

You'll get a look at Formatted Memo and Graphic fields in Chapter 4. The *Binary*, *Short Number*, and *OLE* field types are decidedly beyond the scope of this book.

In the present example, you'll use only Alphanumeric fields, which can contain any combination of characters and spaces. You'll get a closer look at the other data types before this chapter is over.

To define a field as Alphanumeric, select Alphanumeric, or type an A in the Field Type column. You don't have to enter the A in uppercase, but Paradox will display it uppercase regardless.

Field Size

When you've entered the field type, press [Tab⇕] or [↵Enter], and you'll move to the Size column. You must specify a size for Alphanumeric and Memo type fields, which can contain up to 255 or 240 characters, respectively. In this field, type 15. When you choose another data type, the cursor goes directly to the next line in the Field Name column because numeric and currency fields take their width from the data you enter into them. However, if a numeric or currency value contains more digits than its field is formatted for (allowing for a decimal point and two decimal places), it may not appear on the screen exactly as you enter it.

When you enter the field size, you have completed the definition of the first field. Press `Tab⇥` or `⏎Enter` twice to skip the Key column and continue.

Paradox creates a new record below the first, with the record number 2. Continue with this table, entering the following field names, types, and sizes:

First name	A	15
Company	A	30
Address 1	A	30
Address 2	A	20
City	A	20
State	A	2
Zip code	A	10
Phone number	A	14

When you're finished, your screen should look like Figure 3.4.

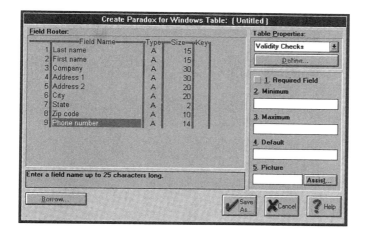

Figure 3.4
Completing the definition of the ROLODEX table.

Why use only Alphanumeric fields? After all, Zip codes and phone numbers are numbers. But consider what would happen with numbers such as nine-digit Zip codes, phone numbers formatted with parentheses and hyphens, or Social Security numbers.

The only characters that can be entered into Numeric fields are digits and arithmetic operators. Neither Paradox nor your computer makes any distinction between a hyphen and a minus sign. They are, for all intents and purposes, the same character. Paradox will let you enter a set of parentheses in a phone number, or the first hyphen in a Social Security number, because it interprets these symbols as indicating a negative number.

However, if you try to enter a phone number in the form *(408)555-0830*, Paradox will display the message Invalid charac- ter and will refuse to let you leave the field until you have corrected the entry. It doesn't know how to interpret the result as a number. Also, Paradox routinely strips off leading zeros. Thus, you'd have trouble with Zip codes and Social Security numbers beginning with 0. (You'd have even more trouble with British Commonwealth postal codes such as *J8W 1C4*).

How were the widths of our Alphanumeric fields chosen? If Paradox will allow Alphanumeric fields of up to 255 characters, why not make them all the maximum length? Why impose any limitation at all? The reason is that Paradox allocates storage space, both in your computer's memory and on disk, for the number of characters you specify. Even if a field contains only two characters, Paradox still reserves space for the number of charac- ters specified in the field type definition. Thus, you have to balance your computer's resources against the form of the data you expect to enter.

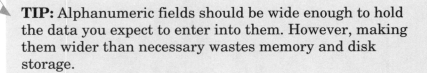

TIP: Alphanumeric fields should be wide enough to hold the data you expect to enter into them. However, making them wider than necessary wastes memory and disk storage.

Saving the Table Structure

Now that you've created your database definition, save it by selecting the Save As... button. You'll see the Save Table As dialog box illustrated in Figure 3.5. As you can see, Paradox will save the table in whatever directory you've specified as the work directory. Enter the name `Rolodex` and press ⏎Enter or select OK. The window will close, leaving you with an empty desktop.

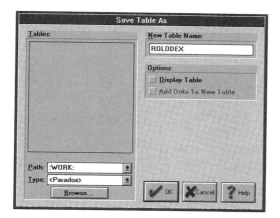

Figure 3.5
The Save Table As dialog box.

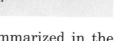

TIP: If you want to work with the table immediately after you've created it, click the Display Table box.

The procedure for creating a table is summarized in the following Quick Steps:

Creating a Table

1. Select File New Table or right-click on the table speedbar icon and choose New. | Paradox displays the Table Type dialog box.

2. Select OK. | Paradox creates a Field Roster window in which you define the fields.

continues

continued

3. Type a field name and press `Tab⇆`, `↵Enter`, or `→` to move to the next column.

The cursor moves to the Field type column.

4. Enter a data type: A, M, N, $, or D. Move to the next column.

The cursor moves to the Size column.

5. If the field is an Alphanumeric or Memo type field, enter a size of up to 255 or 240 respectively. Move to the next column.

The cursor moves to the Key column.

6. If the field is to be a key field, double-click or press `Spacebar`. Press `Tab⇆`, `↵Enter`, or `→`. (See Chapter 5 for more on key fields.)

7. Repeat steps 3 through 6 until all fields are defined.

8. Select Save As....

Paradox creates a table with the structure you have defined and clears the desktop.

TIP: When the desktop is empty, you can right-click on the leftmost button on the speedbar and choose New to execute the File New Table command.

Viewing Tables

When you create a table, the workspace clears itself (unless you checked the **D**isplay Table box). To enter data in your newly created database, you must have the table on the desktop.

Select the File Open Table command or click on the leftmost button on the speedbar. A dialog box will appear, with a list area. As Figure 3.6 shows, you have a choice of two tables, STRUCT.DB and ROLODEX.DB.

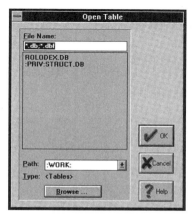

Figure 3.6
Selecting a table to view.

NOTE: STRUCT is a special table containing all the information you entered when you created the table. It is a temporary table, which Paradox will reuse when you create a new table. Notice also that the table name is preceded by the name :PRIV:. This is an *alias* for your private directory—the directory Paradox uses for its working files. If you don't remember what an alias is, review Chapter 2.

If you're on a network, it's very important for you to have a private directory to which no one else has access. If you don't, any temporary files that Paradox creates for you may be replaced by other people's temporary files, which can become very confusing.

To view your new table, select it from the list. When you've selected the table, it will appear in your workspace, as shown in Figure 3.7. It has no records in it, because you haven't entered any. You'll notice that when the table window arrived on the desktop, several new commands appeared on the menu, and the speedbar also acquired a different set of icons. You'll notice both the menu and the speedbar change according to what's displayed in the active window.

As the window title indicates, you're now in View mode, viewing a table in your working directory. (The latter is indicated by the fact that the title bar shows only the type of window you're looking at [Table] and the filename. If you open a file from another directory, the title bar will also include an alias or a pathname.) You can't see the entire table, only the first few fields, because the table is too wide to fit onto the screen. However, that will change once you begin entering data.

Figure 3.7
An empty table.

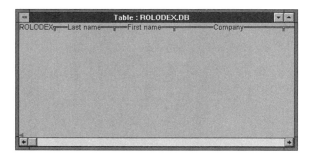

Viewing Several Tables

You can view more than one table at a time, or several copies of the same table at the same time. To try this, select the File Open Table command, and select the ROLODEX table again. You'll now see two copies of the ROLODEX table. They'll be exactly the same. However, the second version appears on top of the first, hiding everything but the window title of the first copy.

Whenever you add a table to the workspace, it appears on top of the currently selected table, in a *cascaded* arrangement. Also, the second table's title bar is highlighted, indicating that this copy of the table is currently selected.

Try adding another table to the workspace. Select File Open Table again, and select STRUCT. Press ⏎Enter or click OK.

As you can see from the highlighting and the position of the cursor, the STRUCT table is now selected. You can see this arrangement in Figure 3.8.

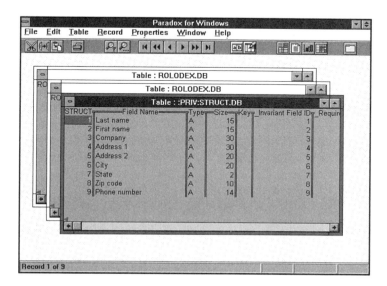

Figure 3.8
Three cascaded windows.

As long as it's on the desktop, take note of a few other things about the STRUCT table. You can see the data you entered, in other words, the fields you created, and the four columns that appeared in the field roster. But there are also some additional fields to the right. These fields can contain information that you might enter in other areas of the window containing the Field Roster. You'll learn about these items later.

Moving Within a Table

The STRUCT table functions in all respects like any other Paradox table, even though the only data it contains comprises the information you entered to create the ROLODEX table. Since it's selected and has some records in it—records containing descriptions of the fields in your ROLODEX table—try moving around in it. You can do this with the keyboard, the mouse, menu commands, or the speedbar.

Moving Around Using the Keyboard

Try pressing ↓. You'll see the cursor move down in the current column until it reaches the bottom.

Experiment with these keys:

You'll find they all move the cursor around in the table. You'll see a message on the status line at the bottom of the screen of the form:

Record *n* of *m*

This tells you how many records are in the table, and which record is current. The number in the position of the *n* changes as you move up and down through the table. Table 3.2 summarizes all of the cursor-movement keys. They can be used when you're viewing a table from the main menu, creating a table, or editing a table.

Table 3.2
Cursor-Movement Keys for Creating, Viewing, or Editing a Table

Key	Effect
⇧Shift+Tab⇆, ←	Moves left one field. If in the first field, moves to the last field of the previous record.
→, Tab⇆, ⏎Enter	Moves right one field. If in the last field, moves to the first field of the next record.
↓	Moves to the current field in the next record. When editing, creates blank records when at the end of the table.
↑	Moves to the current field in the previous record.
Home	Moves to the first field of the current record.

Key	Effect
End	Moves to the last field of the current record.
Ctrl + Home	Moves to the first field in the first record.
Ctrl + End	Moves to the last field in the last record.
PgDn	Moves to the last record or moves the cursor one window down.
PgUp	Moves to the first record or moves one window up.
Ctrl + Z	Finds a specific item in the current field.
Ctrl + A	Finds the next instance of a given item in the current field.
Ctrl + F11	Moves to the first record in the table.
Ctrl + F12	Moves to the last record in the table.
F11	Moves to the previous record in the table.
F12	Moves to the next record in the table.

Moving Around Using the Mouse

To move around in a table with the mouse, you use the *scroll bars* along the right and bottom edges of the table. You don't have a scroll bar on the right side of the window now, because all the records fit in the window. But if you were to make the window smaller, or add records to the table, a scroll bar would appear.

Moving Around Using the Menu

In addition to the cursor keys and the mouse, the commands on the **R**ecord menu can help you move quickly through your table. You'll see this menu in Figure 3.9. The commands on this menu are largely self-explanatory. As you can see, you can move to the **F**irst or **L**ast record in your table, or the record before or after the current one (with the **P**revious and **N**ext commands). The Ne**x**t Set and Pre**v**ious Set commands are equivalent to PgDn and PgUp, respectively.

Figure 3.9
The Record menu.

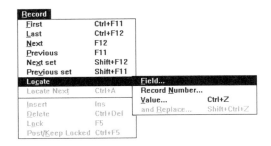

There's also a Locate command on this menu. This command lets you search for a specific value or a specific field, rather than move to a specific record defined by its location. Try it now—select Record Locate Value.... You'll see the dialog box shown in Figure 3.10. You'll search in the Field Name field, which is already selected in the list box, so you needn't do anything to the list box. Just type name in the Value entry field, and press ↵Enter) or click OK. You'll see the highlight move to the entry Last name. Now select Record Locate Next, or just press Ctrl+ A). The highlight will move to the next instance of the text, the First name entry.

Figure 3.10
The Locate Value dialog box.

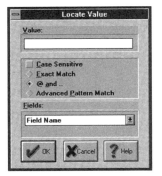

As you can see, you needn't search for the first text that appears in a record. Paradox will find the text anywhere in the field. You also needn't match the case of the text to be searched for, unless you check the Exact Match box.

> **TIP:** You can also use the Record Locate command to search for a specific field or for a record by number.

Being able to go directly to a field by name isn't much help when you have a table of only a few columns, but think again of your Rolodex table. Only three fields show on the screen. If you wanted to move quickly to the State field, this would be the quickest way to get there.

You'll learn other ways to get around in a table when you begin entering and editing data.

Moving Around Using the Speedbar

When a table is on the screen, the speedbar takes the form shown in Figure 3.11. As you can see, the buttons in the leftmost block all duplicate commands on the Record menu. When the mouse pointer rests on one of these buttons, the menu command it executes appears on the status line at the bottom of the desktop. To use these shortcuts, just click on the appropriate button.

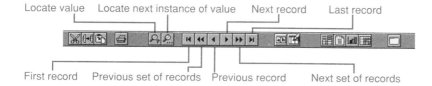

Figure 3.11
The table window speedbar.

Renaming, Copying, and Deleting Tables

Paradox provides tools for renaming, copying and deleting tables. All are on the **F**ile **U**tilities submenu, shown in Figure 3.12.

Figure 3.12
The Table Utilities submenu.

Renaming a Table

You use the File Utilities Rename command to rename an existing table. This saves the table in a new file with a new name, as
shown in the following Quick Steps.

Renaming a Table

1. Select File Utilities
Rename.

Paradox displays the
Rename dialog box.

2. Select the table from the
Table list box. If it's not
there, select its directory
from the Path list box first,
or type its name, including
its alias or path name. Or,
select Browse and use the
directory tree diagram to
locate it.

Paradox enters the name
in the From field, and
moves the cursor to the
To field.

3. Type in the new name for the table, including the .DB extension. To have either the original or the duplicate table appear on the desktop, click the appropriate box.

Paradox renames the table and all associated files.

As an exercise, select the STRUCT table and enter the new name: `rolodx_s`. Nothing will happen of any interest at present.

NOTE: The **F**ile **U**tilities **R**ename command renames all the files that make up a table, as well as the table itself.

Copying a Table

The **T**able **U**tilities submenu also includes a command to copy tables. You can practice this command now. To copy a table, use the following Quick Steps:

Copying a Table

1. Select **F**ile **U**tilities **C**opy. Paradox displays the Copy dialog box.

2. Select the table from the Table list box, or use the Path list box or Browse to find and select the table.

Paradox enters the name in the From field and moves the cursor to the To field.

continues

continued

3. Type in the new name for the table, including the .DB extension. If you want either the original or the duplicate table to appear on the desktop, click the appropriate box. Paradox creates a second table, identical to the original table.

If you had already entered data into the table, the data as well as the table structure would be copied.

You can practice this command now. You'll copy your ROLODEX table, and later you'll delete the copy. Follow the steps just given to copy Rolodex to a table named Temp.

NOTE: The **F**ile **U**tilities **C**opy command copies all the files that make up a table, as well as the table itself. However, it doesn't copy files such as form and report files that go with the table.

Deleting a Table

To delete a table, follow these Quick Steps:

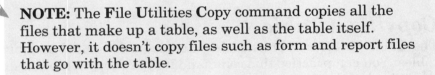

Deleting a Table

1. Select **F**ile **U**tilities **D**elete.

Paradox displays the Delete dialog box.

2. Select the table from the Table list box, or use the Path list box or Browse to find and select the table.

Paradox enters the name in the Delete File field.

3. Select the OK button.	Paradox deletes the table and all associated files.

The Temp table you created earlier for practice is not needed. Delete it by using the steps just given. Delete the rolodx_s table as well.

NOTE: You should always use Paradox menu commands to copy, rename, or delete tables, rather than Windows or DOS commands. If you use Windows or DOS commands, you probably will fail to include in the operation some of the files that make up the table.

Borrowing a Structure

Even though you haven't entered any data in your Rolodex table yet, you can borrow its structure for a new table. This will let you try out your knowledge of data types and use the **B**orrow command.

You'll use a variation on the structure of the ROLODEX table to begin the order-entry application. Use the File New Table command to get a new Create window. You're going to create a new table named CUSTOMER and borrow the structure for it from the one named ROLODEX. The following Quick Steps show how to borrow a table structure:

Borrowing a Table Structure

1. Select File New Table.	Paradox creates the blank structure table in which you'll define your new table.

continues

continued

2. Select Borrow (on the button near the bottom of the window).

Paradox displays a list of tables in the working directory.

3. Select the table whose structure you want to borrow, and select OK.

Paradox copies the field roster from the selected table into the Create window, starting at the position where the cursor was when you invoked the **B**orrow command. You can now add, delete, or edit field names, types, and sizes anywhere in this field roster.

4. Select the Save as... button, type the name of your new table in the **N**ew **T**able Name field, and press ⏎Enter) or select OK.

Paradox asks you to enter the name of a table to create.

CAUTION   The table whose structure you want to borrow may not be in the current directory. If this is the case, you'll need to type the name of its directory in the Path field, or use the Browse button and select the desired directory.

Hints on Borrowing Table Structures

You can borrow the structure of more than one table if you need to create a table that contains fields common to several. You can thus make sure that both tables with the same fields use the same field names, types, and sizes.

Also, you can borrow a table structure at any point while creating a new table. The borrowed structure will appear beginning in the row where the cursor is located. Later, when you've created several linked tables, you'll learn some uses for borrowing from more than one table structure.

To borrow only part of a table structure, delete the field definitions you don't need by moving the cursor to the rows in which they appear and pressing Ctrl+Del.

Editing a STRUCT Table

In the ROLODEX table, you are free to include or leave out any information in a given record. In the customer database, however, you need complete address information, so you know where to ship the goods you sell. Let's add a department address. Move the cursor to the first column, next to field number 1 and follow these steps:

1. Move the cursor to the Company field name in the Field Name column.

2. Press Ins to make room for a new field name.

3. Type Department.

4. Press Tab⇄, →, or ↵Enter to move to the Type column.

5. Type A and press ↵Enter.

6. Press Tab⇄, →, or ↵Enter to move to the Size column.

7. Type 20 and press ↵Enter.

Now let's change the names of the Address fields:

1. Move the cursor to the Address 1 field name.

2. Press F2 to go into field view.

3. Delete the last two characters of the field name with ←Backspace.

4. Press Home to move to the beginning of the field.

5. Type `Street` followed by a space.

6. When you're finished, press `F2` to leave field view.

7. Move down to the Address 2 field.

8. Type `Suite no. or P.O. box`. (Because the entire field name is highlighted, the old name disappears as soon as you begin to type.)

9. Move down to the Zip code field name.

10. Press `F2` to enter field view.

11. Use `Ctrl`+`←` (or click the mouse) to move to the c in the word code.

12. Type `or postal`, followed by a space.

13. Press `F2` to leave field view.

14. Move down one more line and press `Ins`.

15. Type `Country`.

16. Press `Tab`, `→`, or `↵Enter` to move to the Type column.

17. Type `A`.

18. Press `Tab`, `→`, or `↵Enter` to move to the Size column.

19. Type `12` and press `↵Enter`.

(As long as we're setting up a hypothetical business, we might as well make it a big one!)

Now you'll use some new data types. Move to the last line of the structure table, which should now be record 12. The cursor will automatically move back to the Field Name column. Type the following field information:

```
Credit limit            $
```

Now press `↓` to move to record 13, and enter the following:

```
Initial order           D
```

Remember, you can press Tab⇅, ⏎Enter, or → to move from one entry field to the next. If you mistype a field type indicator, Paradox beeps softly and refuses to accept your entry. You can always select your data type from the list by clicking the right mouse button or pressing Spacebar.

You've now established a Currency-type field and a Date-type field. Your field roster should look like Figure 3.13. Select Save as... to save your work, and name your new table CUSTOMER.

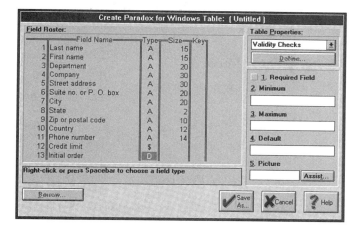

Figure 3.13
The completed CUSTOMER table definition.

You're not entirely through with the structure of the CUS-TOMER table yet. However, leave it for now until you've learned some more advanced concepts. In Chapter 6, you'll modify it using the File Utilities Restructure command.

Edit Mode

1. Bring the table to the desktop.
2. Press F9, click the Edit button on the speedbar, or choose Table Edit Data.
3. Enter the data in each record.
4. Press F9.

Insert a Record

- In Edit mode, press Ins.

Delete a Record

- In Edit mode, press Ctrl + Del.

Search for a Value

1. Press Ctrl + Z or click on the Search Value button.
2. Enter the value to search for.
3. Select the field in which to search.
4. Press ↵Enter or click on OK.
5. Press Ctrl + A to search for the value again.

4

Entering and Editing Data

Now you have created a database table, but there is no data in it. Before you can begin managing data and extracting useful information from it, you must have some data to work with. You can enter data into your Paradox tables in two different types of windows. In addition, you can transfer data from one table to another. This chapter introduces you to entering data, and you'll get your first look at a form.

Entering Data

You're going to enter data into the ROLODEX table you created in Chapter 3. If the table isn't already on the desktop, click the Table icon. Select ROLODEX.DB from the list and choose OK.

Your screen should now look like Figure 4.1. As you can see, the table is empty, because you haven't entered any data into it.

You enter information the same way you did when you were filling out the Field Roster. You use the same keys to move through the table. Now, however, you're going to enter some data into your ROLODEX table. Press F9 or click the Edit button on the speedbar to switch from View to Edit mode. You'll notice several changes to the table and to the screen, as illustrated in Figure 4.2.

Figure 4.1
An empty table.

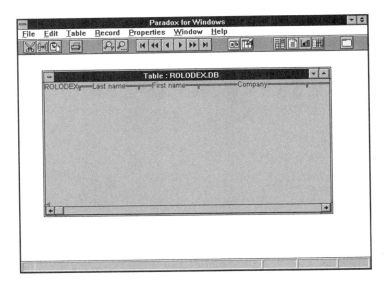

Figure 4.2
Entering Edit mode.

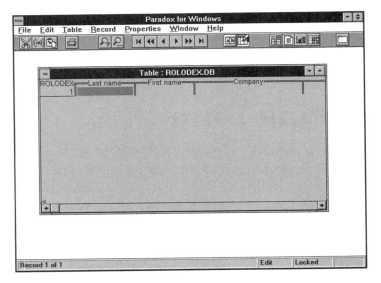

First, a record number appears in the leftmost column. Second, the first field of the first record is now highlighted. (This will be true whether or not there is any data in the table.) As is usual with Windows programs, this means that the entire field is selected. As soon as you press a key that produces a character, whatever is highlighted (in this case, nothing) will disappear and the character you typed will replace it.

At the bottom of the screen, note the changes in the status bar. In one of the boxes at the right, the legend Edit appears, reminding you that you're in Edit mode, and that any keys you press may change the data in the table. As soon as you press a text key, you'll see the word Locked appear to the right of that legend. This means that the record you're working in (which is specified at the left on the status bar) cannot be accessed by anyone else on your network—or by another copy of Paradox running on your computer. Locking ensures that two people can't make changes to the same record at the same time, thereby corrupting the data.

Your first record will contain the following information:

Frank R. Osterlund
Nationwide Thimsfrabble Co.
7984 Charter Avenue
South China, FL 32378
(904)303-9812

Remember, however, that the individual items have to be appropriate to the fields in which you enter them. So, for example, you won't type the entire name into the Last name field. (If you make typing mistakes, you can use ⬅Backspace to delete characters to the left of the cursor, and make the corrections.) When you finish typing a field entry, press Tab↹, ⬐Enter, or → to move to the next field. After you fill in the first four fields, the database will scroll to show the next field in the table when you press Tab↹, ⬐Enter, or →. Following are the entries you need to make in each field:

Field	Entry
Last name	Osterlund
First name	Frank R.

Field	*Entry*
Company	`Nationwide Thimsfrabble Co.`
Address 1	`7984 Charter Avenue`
Address 2	Skip by pressing Tab ⇄
City	`South China`
State	`FL`
Zip code	`32378`
Phone number	`(904)303-9812`

NOTE: Remember, it's best not to use a middle name or Middle initial field because there are many ways people combine names and initials. Therefore, type both the first name and the middle initial into the First name field. On the other hand, you might want separate First name and Initial fields if you want to use the data in a mailmerged letter. You'd no doubt prefer the salutation *Dear Frank* to *Dear Frank R.*

The right four columns of your database should now look like Figure 4.3. Press ↵Enter (or Tab ⇄ or →)) and you'll be ready to enter your second record, as shown in Figure 4.4. Notice that when the cursor leaves record 1, the legend at the left of the status line *may* change to `Record is posted`. This indicates that, as you leave the record, it is written to disk. It is unlocked and is now available to anyone (or any other copy of Paradox) who may want to view or change it.

TIP: You can always enter another record after you complete one, because Paradox creates a blank record when the cursor moves past the end of the current record.

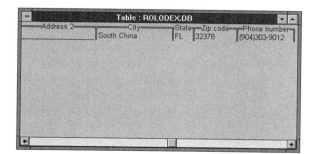

Figure 4.3

A database with one completed record.

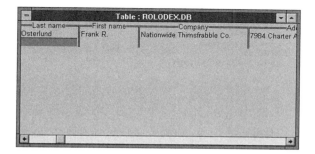

Figure 4.4

Ready to enter the second record.

Now type the second record. See if you can do it without guidance, but remember to skip past empty fields. You'll know a field should be empty because there will be a blank line among the items to be entered. In the following record, there is again no second address:

Johnson
J. Josiah
Daily Bugle
1 Bugle Plaza
New York
NY
10001
(212)500-9000

Using Form View

For the third record, try something different: This time you'll enter the data into a *form*. Press ⌐F7⌐ (the *Quick Form* key) or click the Quick Form button on the speedbar. Paradox will then create a window whose title bar briefly flashes Form Design:New while Paradox creates the form, and then changes to Form:New [Data Entry].

This Standard form is the default form which Paradox creates automatically for any table. The resulting form is shown in Figure 4.5.

Figure 4.5

A Paradox Standard (default) form.

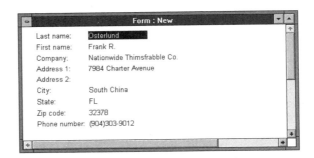

Study this screen before you proceed. First, note that information displayed on the screen has changed. The status bar reads [:WORK:ROLODEX.DB], which tells you the name of the table with which the form is associated. (A form must always be associated with, and based on, a table.)

Look at the form window again. Within the window appears all the information from a single record of your table. The status bar still tells you which record is on view, and how many are in the table. The field names, instead of being arranged across the top of the table, are now in a column at the left margin of the screen. The entry areas are to the right of the field names, instead of below them. The current field is indicated by the highlight bar.

Try moving down and up through the form with ⌐↓⌐ and ⌐↑⌐. Notice that the highlight moves in a vertical line. Both the field names and the data are neatly lined up in columns.

Enter the next record using this form. Press F9 or click the Edit button on the speedbar, and press PgDn twice to get to the third record. (If you left the highlight on a field other than Last name, press Home to get to the top of the form.) Enter the following data in the next record, pressing ↓ after each entry:

```
Khorajian
Corey
Khorajian Plating & Welding Co.
1923 Chascarillo Avenue
P.O. Box 985
Palomar
CA
90006
(619)906-5432
```

When you move on to the Company field, you'll find that you can't enter anything after the Co. Remember, you defined the field as being 30 characters wide. The period is the 31st character. You can't enter the period, because there's no room for it. (Now you know why your name is sometimes spelled funny on bulk-mailed advertisements.) If you want to widen the field, see "Changing a Field's Characteristics" in Chapter 6. Or you can simply live with the limitation.

Cursor Movement in Form Windows

You can still use Tab and ↵Enter to move to the next field, as in table windows; ⇧Shift + Tab and ↑ move to the previous field, as before. But there are some differences.

In the form you've created with the Quick Form key, all fields are in a vertical column. However, if you create a form for a table with many more fields, the default form will arrange the fields in two columns, "wrapping" long fields to fill as many lines as needed. And in a custom form, you can place fields anywhere on the screen. When the fields are not arranged vertically, pressing ↓ moves the cursor to the first field on the line *below* the current field, even if there are other fields on the same line. And Tab and ↵Enter move the cursor to the right if there's a field to the right, zigzagging back and forth across the form. You reach other fields on the current line with ← or →.

TIP: In Chapter 11, you'll learn how to design a form in which you can control the order in which the Tab key moves through fields.

For reference, the keys that move the cursor through a form and their effects are summarized in Table 4.1. For now, continue to type the data for Corey Khorajian. Remember to place the City, State, and Zip code into separate fields.

Table 4.1
Special Keys Used in Form Windows

Key	Moves
⇧Shift + Tab⇆	To the previous field. If in the first field of a record, moves to the last field of the previous record.
Tab⇆, ↵Enter	To the next field. If in the last field of a record, moves to the first field of the next record. In a two-column form, moves to the nearest record, regardless of column.
↓	Down one field.
↑	Up one field.
Home	To the first field in the current record.
End	To the last field in the current record. If in a two-column form, moves to the last field in the first column of the current record.
Ctrl + Home	To the first field of the first record.
Ctrl + Esc	To the last field of the last record. In a two-column form, moves to the last field in the first column of the last record.
PgDn	To current field in previous record.
Ctrl + ↓	To the current field in the last record.
PgUp	To current field in next record.
Ctrl + ↑	To the current field in the first record.
Ctrl + PgUp	Moves the form to the left within the window.
Ctrl + PgDn	Moves the form to the right within the window.
Ctrl + Z	Finds a specific item in the current field.

Key	Moves
Ctrl + A	Finds the next instance of a given item in the current field.
Shift + any cursor key	Highlights the text across which the cursor moves for deleting, cutting, or copying.

When you finish typing the phone number, press Home, then PgDn. You should be at the beginning of record 4, as indicated on the status bar. Now enter a fourth record, using the form. Again, try to enter it on your own. Use the following information:

```
Joy
Anne
Deli Delights
3498 Park Avenue South
New York
NY
10023
(212)555-0000
```

The Ditto Key

For your fifth and sixth records, you'll use a data-entry shortcut: the *Ditto* key. Whether you're in a form window or table window, Ctrl + D automatically copies the information in a given field from the same field in the previous record. Type the following data in Form view:

```
Darnell
Andrew
Creole Kids, Ltd.
1567 E. 83rd Street
New York
NY
10058
(212)112-9009
```

Type the first four fields as usual. Skip the fifth. When you come to the sixth field, City, press Ctrl+D. The text New York appears in the entry field.

Move to the next field and press Ctrl+D again. The text NY appears. Move to the next field, and press Ctrl+D again. The Zip code 10023 appears. This isn't the Zip code you want, but you may find it easier to edit the field than to type the entire Zip code. First press F2 to remove the highlight (or the entire field will be erased). Then press +Backspace twice to enter the correct digits.

Now try entering the phone number with Ctrl+D. It's not the right phone number, but it includes some of the characters you want to use. Edit this field using Field view. Press Ctrl+F or F2, or click the Field View icon on the speedbar to enter Field view. Now follow these steps:

1. Press Home to move the cursor to the beginning of the field.

2. Press → (5 times) or click after the closing parenthesis to move the cursor to the first digit after the closing parenthesis.

3. Press ⇧Shift+→ or drag to the end of the field to highlight the rest of the field.

4. Type 112-9009 to enter the new phone number.

5. Press F2 to leave Field view.

Now try the Ditto key in the table window. Press F7 (the Quick Form key) again, or click the Table button on the speedbar. Your screen will again display the ROLODEX table as a table.

TIP: Once you have created a form, you can switch between the table window and the form window at will by pressing F7 or clicking the Table and Quick Form buttons on the speedbar for the other type of window.

Press ⏎Enter to begin the next record and type the following information:

```
Schocks
Susan
International Footwear
503 E. 23rd Street
New York
NY
10034
(212)555-1357
```

Once again, use Ctrl + D to enter the City, State, and Zip code. Don't forget to edit the last two digits of the Zip code. You'll see the data appear in the table directly below the equivalent entries in the previous record. You'll see three similar entries in these fields, as Figure 4.6 shows.

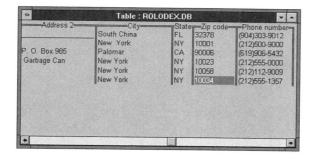

Figure 4.6

The effect of the Ditto key.

To complete the table, add four more records, for an even 10. Add the data for the following records, either in Table view or in Form view. You might even use F7 to switch between them for different records.

Be careful to place the information into the correct fields—these entries aren't pre-arranged to fit into the proper field, as the others were. Remember that if you make mistakes, you can edit a field in Field view, or delete the entire contents of a field using Ctrl + ◆Backspace. Also, be alert for places where you can use Ctrl + D, the Ditto key. Here are the entries:

```
Susan Lathom
Sky High Technologies
11200 Dakota Avenue
Fresno, CA 94371
(209)901-6021

Howard K. Franklin
Sky High Technologies
11200 Dakota Avenue
Fresno, CA 94371
(209)901-6027

James E. Jones
Empire Sound
3994 Sepulveda Avenue
Suite 901N
Hollywood, CA 91733
(213)404-4400

Y. B. Normal
New String Arts
1984 Jordan Road
Cannon Beach, OR 97110
(503)502-6767
```

When you're done, press F9 or click the Edit button on the speedbar to leave Edit mode. The following Quick Steps summarize the procedure for entering data.

Entering Data in a Table or Form

1. Bring the table or form to the desktop.

2. Press F9 or click the Edit button.

The word Edit appears on the status bar.

3. Enter the data in the appropriate fields.

4. Press F9 or click the Edit button to leave edit mode.

Editing Tables

It's easy to edit an existing table. When you edit an existing table you can perform several functions:

- Delete or edit fields in existing records.
- Insert new records into the table at any point.
- Delete complete records from the table.
- Append (add) new records to the end of the table.

Since you've already got the ROLODEX table on the desktop, let's edit it. Press [F9] or click the speedbar Edit button to enter Edit mode. The status bar will reflect the change.

Appending Records to a Table

Now append some records to the end of the table. You should already be in record 10. Press [PgDn] to move to the last record and [↓] to create a new, blank record.

Add the data for the following record:

```
Norma Loquendi
True Recordings
1030 South Street Suite 10
Beaverton, OR 97005
(503)555-0101
```

When you finish that record, press [Tab↹] or [↵Enter]. Notice that when you append records, Paradox creates new records for you to fill in, just as it did when you created the table.

NOTE: When you leave Edit mode, Paradox automatically deletes any blank records from the end of the table.

Add the following record:

```
James Jones
5110 West End Avenue
Brooklyn, NY 11267
(718)903-4912
```

Inserting Records into a Table

Press Ctrl + Home to move to the first record. For the first time, your cursor enters the Record number field. You can't edit this field, as you'll find out if you press an alphanumeric key. But what if you want to change a record number?

As a rule, it's best to regard record numbers as arbitrary. However, you can create a new record with a given number. To create a new record 3, for example:

1. Press ↓ twice to move to record 3.

2. Press Ins to create a new record at this position.

All the other records will move down on the screen, with their numbers increased by 1, as Figure 4.7 shows.

Figure 4.7

Inserting a record into a table.

Paradox creates a blank line for the new record.

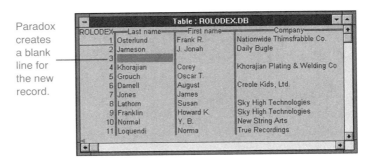

If you haven't pressed any other keys, your cursor should still be in record 3 in the Last name column. Now try pressing ↑ to move the cursor up to the second record. Notice that the blank record disappears, and the record below it moves up to fill the space. If you inadvertently create a blank row (by pressing Ins), Paradox eliminates it. It assumes that others may be updating the same database, and randomly inserted blank rows would cause confusion.

Move down to record 3 and press `Ins` again to re-create the blank row, move down to it, and type the values for the following entry:

```
Jane Jonas
6701 Colonial Road
Apt. 4H
Philadelphia, PA 30067
(714)502-5891
```

TIP: If you need to number your records for some purpose of your own (as you will later with the CUSTOMER table), it's better to create a separate field for this purpose.

When you press `Tab ⁵` or `⏎Enter` at the end of the phone number, you'll find that the cursor has moved to record number 4. If you were to start typing, the name Khorajian, which already occupies the Last name field in record 4, would be deleted and the new characters would replace it. (If you inadvertently added some characters, press `Esc` and the changes will be undone.)

NOTE: You must press `Ins` each time you want to insert a record.

Searching for a Value with the Zoom Key

You can use `Ins` to take advantage of Paradox's ability to copy information from the previous record. To do so, you have to make sure that you're inserting a record after the one containing the information you want to copy.

To do that, you'll use Paradox's searching abilities. Press `Ctrl`+`Z` (the *Zoom* key) or click the Search for field value button on the speedbar. You'll see the dialog box in Figure 4.8. In the Value field, type `Jones`. The Fields list box already displays `Last Name`, so just choose OK. (If you want to search for a value in a different field, simply select it from this list.) The cursor will move to record 3, and the highlight will appear over the last name Jones. Press `Ctrl`+`A` or click the Search Next speedbar button to continue the search. Continuing the Zoom, Paradox moves the cursor to record 10, highlighting Jones again. Press `Ctrl`+`A` until you get the message `"Jones" was not found` at the bottom of your screen. Your search is complete.

Figure 4.8
The Locate Value dialog box.

To use the Ditto key, `Ctrl`+`D`, the information you want to repeat has to be above the current field, just as it does with ditto marks on paper. So you'll now have to move down one more record with `↓`. You don't have to press `Ins`; if you do it's a mess. A blank record will appear after James Jones. Press `Ctrl`+`D`, and `Jones` appears in the field. Press `Tab↹`, and press `Ctrl`+`D` a second time. The name `James` appears in the First name field. Fill out the rest of the record with the following information:

```
Glynphrygh Blivet & Tong Works
91503 Victoria Road
Toronto, ON J1W 7S6
(416)090-4000
```

Using Wild-Card Characters in a Search

You can search for something that resembles the text you want to find, using the wild-card characters @ and .. to find groups of characters that might match what you're looking for. These techniques work with the Zoom command throughout Paradox.

The wild-card character .. represents any characters preceding or following the literal characters you type (somewhat similar to the DOS wild-card character *, but with more flexibility). The @ symbol represents any single character (like the DOS wild-card character ?).

Try these wild-card characters now. Press Ctrl + Z to display the Locate Value dialog box. Enter the value J@n@s in the Value text box. Choose the Last name field from the Fields list box. Make sure @ and .. is selected in the list of options. When you choose OK, you'll see the highlight move to the first instance of Jones. As you press Ctrl + A to continue the search, you'll see the highlight move to the next Jones. After the final Jones, you'll see the NOT FOUND message.

Now try the .. wild-card pattern. Press Ctrl + Z and enter the text ..an.. as the text to search for. Choose the First name field for your search and choose OK. You'll see the Match Found message immediately because the first field contains Frank R., which includes the requested characters. As you press Ctrl + A, the highlight will move to Jane, Anne, Andrew, Susan, and Susan. Notice that this wild-card character can stand for no characters, as well as any number of characters. That's why Paradox found Anne and Andrew, which begin with the requested characters.

Other Ways to Find a Value

You can use Edit mode to modify the data in existing records, as well as to add new ones. Suppose you have just found out the full nine-digit Zip code for *Y. B. Normal* at *New String Arts*. You want to change that record to reflect the new information. Use the power of Paradox to find the information for you and add -1836 to the Zip code. You can use the **R**ecord menu, shown in Figure 4.9.

Figure 4.9
The Record menu.

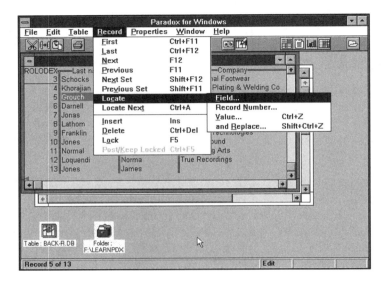

Now follow these Quick Steps to locate the value.

Locating a Specific Value in a Specific Field

1. Choose Record Locate Value.

   Paradox opens the Locate Value dialog box.

2. Enter a known value in the record (in this case `Normal`) and choose OK.

   Paradox finds and highlights the selected item.

3. Choose Record Locate Field.

   Paradox displays the Locate Field dialog box.

> **4.** Press the first letter of the field to locate (in this case, ⌊Z⌋). If more than one field starts with the same letter, keep pressing the letter until the one you want is highlighted. Then choose OK.
>
> The highlight moves to the chosen field in the current record.

This method of finding an item may seem cumbersome when you're working with a small table such as this one, but when a table is larger than the screen in every direction, it can be a great convenience. Now:

1. Press ⌊F2⌋ or click the Field View button to change to Field view, or click the mouse after the 0.

2. Type -1836 to complete the code.

3. Press ⌊F2⌋ or click the Field View button to leave Field view. (You can also press ⌊↵Enter⌋, but that will take you to the next field.)

Special Editing Keys

As you noticed in passing, you can restore changes you made to a field *before you leave it* by pressing ⌊Esc⌋. There are other important editing keys of which you should be aware.

You can still restore changes to a field after you've left it, but *before you've left the record*, by pressing ⌊Alt⌋+⌊←Backspace⌋ or choosing Edit Undo. However, because records are written to disk as soon as the cursor leaves them, you can't undo changes to a record once you've left it.

To delete a record, press ⌊Ctrl⌋+⌊Del⌋ or ⌊Ctrl⌋+⌊←Backspace⌋. But be careful when you do. Once you've deleted a record, there's no way to get it back, even with the Undo key.

Table 4.2 describes the command keys you can use in Edit mode.

Table 4.2
Command Keys in
Edit Mode

Key	Effect
F2	Toggles into and out of Field view.
F9	Exit Edit mode.
Ins	Inserts a new record at the current cursor location, moving the following records down one row (and increasing their record numbers by 1).
Del	Deletes the contents of the current field.
Ctrl+Del	Deletes the current record, moving the cursor up to the previous record (and reducing the record numbers of the following records by 1).
Alt+◆Backspace	Undoes the last change you made to the current record. Successive presses undo previous changes.

Entering Data in Nonalphanumeric Fields

Up to now, we've been working exclusively with Alphanumeric fields. Since the CUSTOMER table has a Currency and a Date field, let's work with that table now. Choose File Open Table, select CUSTOMER.DB from the list, and choose OK. Go into Edit mode. In the course of this exercise, you'll learn a few new things about Date and Numeric values.

Begin entering the following data into the first record of the CUSTOMER table:

```
Pollock
Jack
Production Dept.
Action Designs
3220 Umbrian Way
```

```
Seaside, CA 93732 USA
(408)555-6721
5000
12/12/91
```

The last two items are the Credit limit and the Initial order date.

How Paradox Displays Large Numbers

Now enter another record. This time you'll have to pay special attention to how numbers and dates are displayed, so take it one step at a time. Enter the following values:

```
Jones
Jonathan
Purchasing Dept.
Federated Percussive Effects
900 Harbor Blvd.
Third Floor
Avenel, NJ 07131 USA
(201)555-9332
```

Now look at the Credit limit field of record 1 in Figure 4.10. It's a row of asterisks. Rather than present you with misleading information, Paradox displays asterisks when only part of a field is visible. This is also how Paradox displays numbers that are too large to fit in the allotted space. You have not lost any information.

NOTE: If you want to, you can change the width of columns on the screen. Just drag the right border to the right to widen the column or to the left to narrow it.

Figure 4.10
How Paradox handles large numbers.

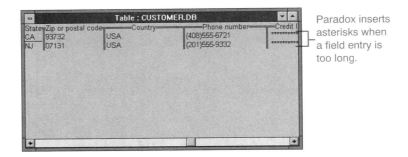

Paradox inserts asterisks when a field entry is too long.

Now press `Tab⇕` or `⏎Enter`. Suddenly, the asterisks disappear, and the entry $5,000.00 replaces it. Here are two peculiarities. First, the number suddenly fits! Second, it's formatted with a dollar sign, a comma, and a decimal point—which you didn't enter—in the appropriate places. Paradox takes its date, number, and currency formats from the defaults established in Windows. Usually, you will have automatically established these defaults when you installed Windows. You can change them using the International section of the Windows Control Panel, but any changes you make there will affect every Windows program you run.

Now type the last two fields for the second record:

8400
Jan.17,1992

After you press `Tab⇕` or `⏎Enter`, press `Ctrl`+`PgDn` three times so that your window looks like Figure 4.11. Notice that the date did not remain in the form in which you typed it. Paradox accepts date entries in any format it can recognize. These include:

011792

1/17/92

1-17-92

Jan1792

Jan171992

Jan.17,92

or virtually any combination that doesn't include spaces and has enough information. If it doesn't understand the form of the date you typed, it will display a message on the status bar explaining the problem and will refuse to let you leave the field.

The default displays formats for dates.

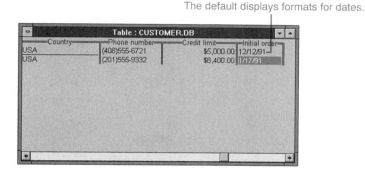

Figure 4.11
Paradox converts the date you enter into the default format.

However, in any given field in a table, the program displays dates in only one format. Paradox has converted the date you typed to the default format. As you'll learn in Chapter 6, Paradox lets you choose one of three formats to use for dates in a table.

Now move your cursor to the field that reads 8,400.00. Try typing 84,00 into the field. Although this is not a legal way to punctuate this value, Paradox cleverly converts it to the proper format.

You now have a CUSTOMER table with two records in it. Press F9 to leave editing mode and choose Window Close All to clear the workspace. Save any changes when asked if you want to do so. Give your form the name rolodex.

Restrictions and Shortcuts for Entering Numeric and Date Values

The last exercise suggests that you may need to know more about ways of entering numbers. You don't have a table with a true Numeric field yet, so you'll create one just for this exercise. Choose File New Table. In the Field Roster, type the following information:

```
Number    N
Date      D
```

Now:

1. Choose Save as.

2. Give the table the name NUMBERS.

3. Check Display table.

4. Choose OK.

Your new table will appear on the desktop.

Restrictions on Numeric Input

In edit mode, type the following numbers, pressing ↓ after each (you'll use the Date field later):

```
987654321
9876543.21
12345.6789
345E102
12,345,678
-12
(500)
```

When you're done, your table should look like Figure 4.12.

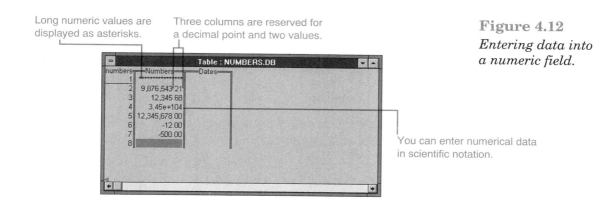

Long numeric values are displayed as asterisks.

Three columns are reserved for a decimal point and two values.

Figure 4.12

Entering data into a numeric field.

You can enter numerical data in scientific notation.

The number in the first record, nine digits long, is too long, but the second, which includes an additional character—a decimal point—fits! What's going on?

It's simple. By default, Paradox reserves three columns in the field for a decimal point and two decimal places. This does not leave enough room to display nine columns to the left of a decimal point. You'll see this is so by looking at record 3. The value in this record also indicates that Paradox rounds off decimal places beyond two.

You don't actually lose any precision, however. If you move the cursor up to record 3 and go into Field view, you can use the arrow keys to see the entire number. Remember to press F2 again when you're through looking at the number.

The fourth record contains an entry in *scientific*, or *exponential, notation*. Paradox both accepts and displays scientific notation. However, by default it places only one digit to the left of the decimal point. Therefore, it adds two to the exponent, signifying two more decimal places.

Next, note that commas have appeared, whether or not you entered any. You'd expect them in record 5, but they are also present in records 2 and 3. As noted, you can enter commas at almost any point, or leave them out. Paradox will format the field according to the national numeric format installed in Windows.

You can choose the format for a numeric field by right-clicking on it to open the Object Inspector and choosing Number Format. You then choose from the following formats:

Windows # The default number format installed in Windows; negative numbers appear with a minus sign.

Windows $ The currency format installed in Windows; negative numbers appear in parentheses.

Fixed Numbers are displayed with the default number of decimal places (usually 2) and no commas; negative numbers appear with a minus sign.

Scientific Exponential notation with one digit before the decimal point; negative numbers appear with a minus sign.

General Numbers appear as they are entered; negative numbers appear with a minus sign.

Comma Numbers formatted with a comma and two decimal places; negative numbers appear in parentheses.

Percent Numbers are increased in value by 100, have one decimal place, and are followed by a percent sign; negative numbers appear with a minus sign.

Integer Numbers rounded to the nearest integer; negative numbers appear with a minus sign.

Note that these formats affect only the display, not the actual value stored. For example, if you enter Field view in Integer format, you'll still see the number of decimal places you entered. Also, numbers entered in scientific notation remain in scientific notation.

Shortcuts for Entering Dates

Move your cursor to the Date field of record 1. Press [Spacebar] three times. You'll see the system date appear. (If you see 1/1/80, you didn't set the date on your computer.) Think of the date as consisting of three subfields:

- Month

- Day

- Year

You can use the Spacebar to enter the current value into any of these subfields. Thus, you could enter a month and a day and press ⸢Spacebar⸥ to enter the current year.

As with Number fields, you can choose the date format from the Object Inspector. You have three choices:

Windows Short   The short number format installed in Windows; commonly this is *mm / dd / yy* and is the default.

Windows Long   The date is fully spelled out (for example, January 17, 1992).

For more details on using the Object Inspector, see Chapter 6.

Sorting Tables

1. Bring the table to be sorted to the desktop and make it current.
2. Choose Table Sort.
3. Choose Same Table or New Table.
4. Select the field(s) to be used as the criteria for the sort. Click the right-arrow button to move those fields to the Sort Order list box.
5. Place the fields in their proper order of priority.
6. Double-click any fields to sort in descending order.
7. Choose Sort.

Correcting Key Violations

1. Select the KEYVIOL table.
2. Press F9.
3. Edit the key fields of each record to make them unique.
4. Choose File Utilities Add.
5. Enter KEYVIOL as the source table.
6. Enter the name of the table from which the records were expelled as the target table.
7. Choose Append, Update, or Append and Update.
8. Choose Add.

Chapter 5

Sorting and Key Fields

When you entered data into your Paradox tables, the records remained in the order in which you entered them. You did some very primitive sorting when you placed one of the Joneses beneath another to take advantage of the Ditto key, Ctrl+D. But using this procedure to enter data into a large table would become quite tedious.

Paradox provides two very different methods for keeping your databases in order:

- A *sort* command.

- A special structural element called a *key*.

In this chapter, you'll learn about both of them.

In a small table such as ROLODEX, it doesn't matter much whether the records are in order. In a full-scale application, however, you might have thousands of records. You'd be hard-pressed to find a specific item if the records weren't sorted in some meaningful way.

Using the Sort Table Dialog Box

In the simplest form of sorting, you just select a single field to be sorted. Paradox quickly rearranges all the records so that the items in the selected field are in ascending (lowest to highest) order. If the fields are Alphanumeric, they are sorted from A to Z. To begin, you'll sort your ROLODEX table on a single field. If anything other than the ROLODEX table is on the desktop, choose Window Close All to clear the desktop. Now click on the Open Table icon on the speedbar and bring the ROLODEX table into the desktop.

To sort a table, you use the Table Sort command to display the Sort Table dialog box, shown in Figure 5.1. Here you specify which field or fields the sort should be based on, and whether the sort should be in *ascending* order or *descending* order.

Figure 5.1

The Sort Table dialog box.

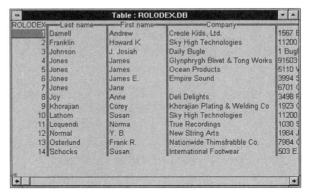

NOTE: *Ascending order* means that text will be sorted alphabetically from A to Z and values will be sorted from smallest to largest. *Descending order* means that text will be sorted from Z to A and values will be sorted from largest to smallest.

Notice that you have several options as to how the result should be handled:

- Same Table places the results in the existing table, over-writing it.

- New Table creates a new table, preserving your original table. You *must* sort to a new table if your table has keys, which you'll learn about shortly.

- Sort Just Selected Fields sorts *only* the designated fields. Any records that have the same values in the fields you choose to sort will have their remaining fields in random order. If you don't check this item, the remaining fields will be sorted in ascending order.

- Display Sorted Table has no effect if you place the sorted records in the same table, because that table must already be on the desktop. If you sort the records to a new table, checking this box displays the new table as well as the old one.

Selecting Fields to Sort

As you can see in Figure 5.1, on the left is a list box labeled **F**ields, containing all the fields in your database. On the right is a list box labeled Sort **O**rder, in which you set up the basis for sorting.

Selecting Fields with the Mouse

To sort the table by one field, select the field from the left box, and click the right-arrow button. This copies the selected field name to the Sort **O**rder box. You can select fields individually, clicking the right-arrow button after each, or select groups of fields at once. To select several fields which appear next to one another, click on the first and drag until all the ones you want are highlighted. Or click the first field, hold down ⇧Shift), and click the last. Then click the right-arrow button.

To sort by several fields whose names are not contiguous, either select one field at a time, clicking the right-arrow button after each, or hold down the Ctrl key, and click on each field to be included as part of the basis for sorting. Then click the right-arrow button.

Selecting Fields with the Keyboard

To select fields for sorting with the keyboard:

1. Use the Tab↹ key to move the highlight to the Fields list box.

2. Press ↓ to highlight the field to sort on.

3. Press Tab↹ to move the highlight to the right-arrow button, and press Spacebar.

4. Press Alt+ F to move back to the Fields list box, and repeat steps 2 and 3 for each additional field to be included in the sort.

A Simple Sort

You'll now sort the file by last name. At this point, there's no reason not to use the same table.

1. Choose Same Table.

2. Move to the Fields list box and select Last name.

3. Click the right-arrow button.

4. Choose OK to complete the procedure.

In a few moments, you'll see the sorted version, as shown in Figure 5.2. (In this and following illustrations, I've maximized the table so you can see more of it.) Since you didn't check Sort Just Selected Fields, the First names are sorted as well.

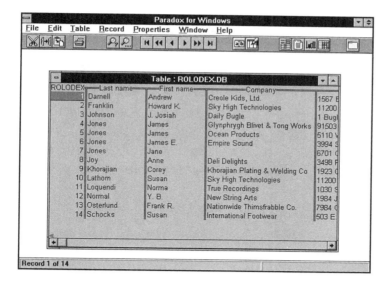

Figure 5.2
The sorted table.

To confirm this point, press F9 or click the Edit button to edit the table, and give James Jones of Glynphrygh Blivet & Tong Works the middle initial W. Now repeat the steps you took to sort the table the first time. You'll see James W. Jones now follows James E. Jones.

Unless you check the Sort Just Selected Fields box, Paradox makes an effort to find the proper place for each record. Try editing the table again. Delete the W. from James W. Jones. Then type the company name `Ocean Products` in the Company field for the James Jones with no company affiliation (record 6). Repeat the sort and you'll see that the two James Joneses are now sorted by company.

A Descending Sort

Now try another sort. This time you'll sort by Company in descending order. Choose Table Sort as before, but this time select the Company field name. To shift to descending order, either double-click the field in the Sort Order box, or click the Sort Direction button. As shown in Figure 5.3, the `123...` at the beginning of the field changes to . . .321, and changes color to signify that you've chosen a descending sort.

Figure 5.3

Setting up a descending sort.

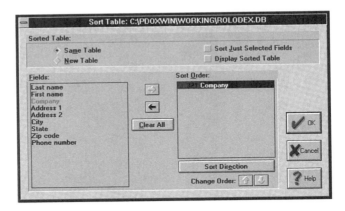

When you choose OK, you'll find that the two employees of Sky High Technologies have been sorted in ascending order, as Figure 5.4 illustrates. (If you think they remained that way because you previously sorted by Last name in *ascending* order, try sorting by Last name in *descending* order and saving the results before you sort by Company.)

Figure 5.4

The table sorted in descending order by Company.

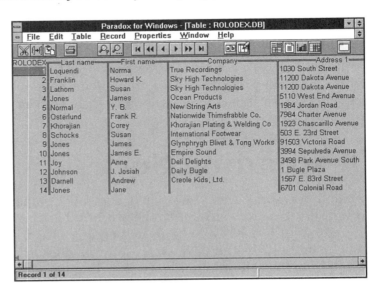

Sorting by Several Fields

You can force Paradox to sort fields other than the primary field in the order you prefer by specifying more than one field in the sorting form. Try sorting your table in descending order by State, and within that, in ascending order by Zip code. If you have more than one entry for the same State and Zip code (which you do in this example), you can force Paradox to put such entries in ascending order by Last name.

To sort by several fields, you first select all the fields to be included in the sort, one at a time or all at once. Then you place them in order of priority by selecting them in the Sort **O**rder box, and clicking the up-arrow and down-arrow buttons until they are in order of priority.

This time you'll sort using four fields and place the result into a second table. You'll be doing exercises later in this chapter that will use this new table. Follow these steps:

1. Choose Table Sort.

2. Choose New Table, and enter the name `rolotemp.db`.

3. Check Display Sorted Table.

4. Select the Last name, First name, State, and Zip code fields, and copy them to the Sort Order list box.

5. Select State and click the up-arrow button twice.

6. Double-click State, or click Sort Direction.

7. Select Zip code and click the up-arrow button twice.

Your sorting form should now look like Figure 5.5.

Notice that you're sorting on three ascending fields and one descending field. By placing the field names in this order, you are specifying that:

- The primary sorting criterion should be State, and states should be sorted in descending order.

- Within states, records should be sorted by Zip code.

- Any records with the same values in the State and Zip code fields should be sorted by Last name.

- Any records that are the same by all three criteria should be sorted by First name.

Figure 5.5

Setting up a sort on several fields.

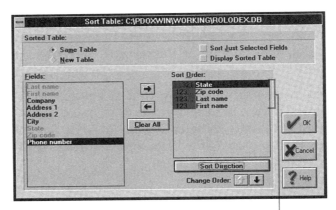

Specifying multiple fields to sort by

Select OK to complete the sort.

Paradox will add the ROLOTEMP table to your desktop on top of the original ROLODEX table. Maximize it by clicking on the arrow in the upper right corner of the window, or by using the Maximize command on the Control menu.

You'll see that the two employees of Sky High Technologies—the only ones sharing a Zip code—are in proper alphabetical order. Now press Ctrl + PgDn to view the State and Zip code fields. Your screen should look like Figure 5.6.

Notice that, as expected, the states are in reverse alphabetical order. If you look at the Zip codes for New York and California, you'll see that they are properly sorted into ascending order within each state. The following Quick Steps summarize the procedure for sorting a table.

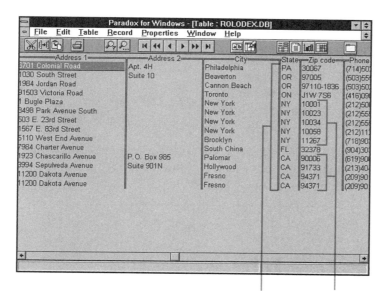

Figure 5.6
A table sorted by several criteria.

States are in reverse alphabetical order.

By state, the Zip codes are sorted in ascending order.

Sorting a Table

QUICK STEPS

1. Choose Table Sort.

Paradox displays the Sort Table dialog box.

2. Choose Same Table or New Table, and enter a name for the sorted file, if a text box appears.

3. Select the field(s) to be used as the criteria for the sort. Click the right-arrow to move those fields to the Sort Order list box.

4. Use the up-arrow and down-arrow keys to place the fields in their proper order of priority.

continues

continued

5. Double-click any fields to
be sorted in descending
order, or select those fields,
one at a time, and click
OK.

6. Choose Sort Direction. To   Paradox sorts the table as
cancel the sort, choose   specified.
Cancel instead.

Key Fields

Now you know how to sort a Paradox database table anyway you
want. But there's a catch. Suppose you add more records to the
table. Unless you carefully place each new record in its proper
position, the new records will be appended to the end of the table.
Paradox keeps no record of your sorting criteria.

You could repeat your sorting procedure each time you enter
data. However, there's a better way.

When you created your first tables in Chapter 3, you saw a
column in the Field Roster labeled Key. If you move the highlight
to that column, this message appears at the bottom of the Field
Roster telling you how to designate a field as a *key field:*

```
Double-click or press any character to set or remove
key;
Keyed fields must be top fields in Field Roster.
```

When you designate a key field, the records for that field are
always sorted in ascending order.

As soon as you move the cursor out of a new or edited record,
Paradox places the new record into its proper place.

But key fields have some restrictions. When you make a field
a key field, Paradox requires that each entry within that field

must be unique. (You can see that those Joneses are going to be a problem.)

Records with the same value in a key field are automatically eliminated from the table, and placed into a separate table called KEYVIOL (for *Key Violation*). This gives you a chance to edit the offending records and reinsert them.

Another restriction is that all key fields must appear in the structure table before any nonkey fields.

Key fields are also the means by which you link the information in one table to information in another, as you'll learn in Chapter 11.

Adding a Key Field to a Table

You can designate a key field when you create a table by placing an asterisk in the Field Type column of the structure table. You can also modify existing table structures and add key fields to them. To try this last method, follow these steps.

Specifying a Key Field

1. Close the table (ROLOTEMP, in this case).

   You'll get an error message if you try to restructure a table that's open.

2. Choose File Utilities Restructure.

3. Select the table (ROLO-TEMP) and choose OK. (You'll deal with ROLO-DEX later.)

   You'll see a window exactly like the one you completed when you created the ROLODEX table. The only difference is the window title: Restructure Paradox for Windows Table: ROLOTEMP.DB.

   continues

continued

4. Move the highlight to the Key column. Follow the directions on the screen to create a key field.

An asterisk will appear in the Key column next to the field (Last name, in this case). This makes it a key field. Your screen should now look like Figure 5.7.

Figure 5.7
Adding a key field to an existing table.

Specifying a key field

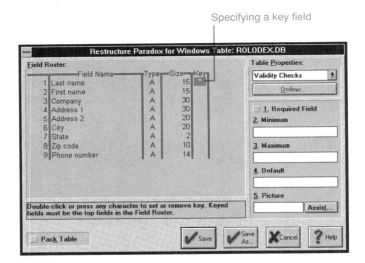

Now choose Save to restructure the ROLOTEMP table. You should see a screen like Figure 5.8.

Notice that both of the James Joneses have been removed from Rolotemp, and the KEYVIOL table is current. This gives you a chance to edit the key field in the offending records and, using the steps described later in this chapter, add the records back into the table.

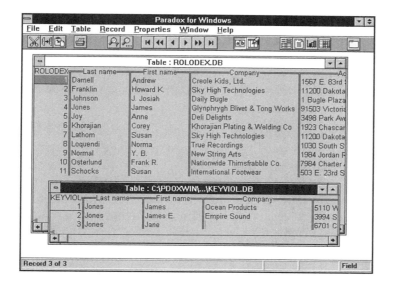

Figure 5.8

*Changes resulting
from adding a key
field to a table.*

NOTE: Nothing about the table itself tells you that it has key fields. The only ways that you can tell a table has key fields are by their consequences—such as the appearance of a KEYVIOL table—or by looking at the structure table.

Adding Several Key Fields

A table can have more than one key field. When it does, the value in any one of the key fields may be nonunique, so long as the combined value of all the items in the key fields of a record differs from the combined value in those key fields in all other records in the table.

Think about what this means in your ROLODEX table. You have three James Joneses. If you were to make both the Last name and First name fields into key fields, you'd have no problem with James E. Jones. But there's nothing to distinguish between the two remaining James Joneses.

Given the limitations regarding key fields, you could make Company into a key field as well. But it's quite possible that there will be several Mary Smiths, say, at a large company. You could make all fields key fields, but that would slow Paradox down somewhat and create serious trouble when you worked with linked tables.

The ideal combination for this table would be Last name, First name, and Phone number. Even in a large company, several employees with the same last and first name would be unlikely to have the same phone number. If necessary, you could widen the Phone number field to include an extension number for those companies where all calls go through a central switchboard. However, the Phone number field isn't next to the First name field, so you can't use it. At least, not yet.

Another approach, one that's very commonly used in database applications, is to create an arbitrary field—such as some kind of ID number—and use that as a key field.

You'll see ways to do both of these things in Chapter 6, when you learn more about how to restructure tables. For now, however, make the Last name and First name fields into key fields.

When you restructure a table more than once, Paradox creates additional KEYVIOL tables, with the names KEYVIOL1.DB, KEYVIOL2.DB, and so on. So you won't lose the info on the Joneses, even if you restructure the table several times. But to be on the safe side, give the table a different name so you'll be able to find it easily. Close the table, then use the File Utilities Rename command to rename the KEYVIOL table to JONESES for the time being. That way, if any more key violations occur, the records now in the KEYVIOL table won't be lost forever.

Proceed with the restructuring:

1. Once again, close the ROLOTEMP table.

2. Choose File Utilities Restructure.

3. Select the ROLOTEMP table and choose OK.

4. When the Restructure window appears, move to the Key column of the First name record, and append another asterisk, as shown in Figure 5.9.

5. Choose Save to complete the task.

As you'll see in Figure 5.10, no new KEYVIOL table has been created, and the records are sorted by last and first name. (I've rearranged the desktop for maximum visibility.)

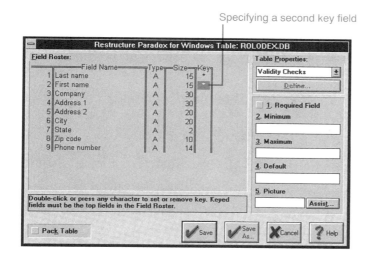

Figure 5.9

Adding a second key field to a table.

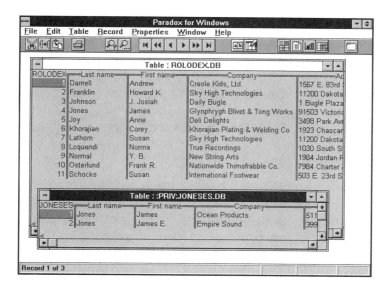

Figure 5.10

A table with two key fields.

Dealing with Key Violations

When two tables have essentially the same structure (not counting key fields), it's easy to add records from one to another. You can use this fact to restore the records from the KEYVIOL table.

Follow these steps to add the JONESES records that were taken from ROLOTEMP:

1. Choose File Utilities Add. You'll see the dialog box in Figure 5.11.

2. Click JONESES.DB to place its name in the text box labeled From.

3. Click in the text box labeled To:.

4. Click ROLOTEMP.DB to transfer its name to that box.

   At this point, you can choose one of three options:

- Append, which adds records to the table, leaving existing records unchanged.

- Update, which only changes the data in existing records.

- Append and Update, which both adds records that have no equivalent in the table, and changes records with the same key values.

If you choose Append and Update, Paradox searches for records with the same key values as the records to be added (in this instance, James Jones or James E. Jones) and replaces all the nonkey fields with fields from the record whose keys match. At the same time, any records that do *not* have the same key values as records in the target table are added.

Since this is a temporary table, go ahead and try it. You'll find that James E. Jones has been properly added to the table. James Jones of Glynphrygh Blivet & Tong Works, however, has replaced James Jones of Ocean Products. Although nothing will tell you so, the record that was changed appears in a table called :PRIV:CHANGED.DB—another temporary table—in your private directory, as the name indicates. Paradox thoughtfully doesn't throw away the data, giving you another chance to make it conform to the standards you've created. Choose File Open Table, and you'll see it in the list. Select it and bring it to the desktop. (There's no Table icon on the speedbar when a table is already open.)

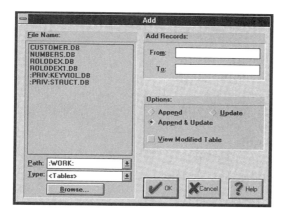

Figure 5.11

Selecting tables for adding records from one table to another.

In Figure 5.12, the tables have been rearranged on the desktop so you can compare the Joneses in the three tables.

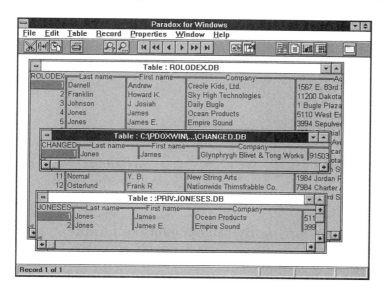

Figure 5.12

Adding and updating records from one table to another.

Restoring Records Eliminated from a Table

1. Make the CHANGED table current and press [F9] or click the Edit button.

2. Edit the records in the CHANGED table so that the values in the key fields, taken together, do not match any values currently in the table. (In this example, go into Field view and change James to James W..)

3. Press [F9] or click the Edit button to end the editing session.

4. Choose File Utilities Add.

    Paradox displays the Table Add dialog box.

5. Choose :PRIV:CHANGED:.DB as the source table.

6. Choose the target table (in this example, ROLOTEMP.DB).

7. Choose Append.

8. Choose OK.

    Paradox adds the edited records to the target table.

When you're done, the table should look like the one in Figure 5.13. All your original records are now back in the ROLOTEMP table, properly sorted.

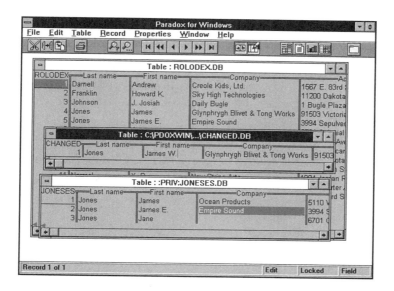

Figure 5.13
Adding changed records back into the source table.

If you cycle through the windows, you'll see that there are still records in the JONESES and CHANGED tables. The records from these tables have been copied, not moved, to the ROLOTEMP table. As you can see, Paradox gives you every opportunity to recover any data that may be eliminated as the result of changes.

Sorting Tables with Key Fields

You can sort tables that have key fields in the same manner as any other table, with one important restriction: You *must* place the sorted data into a different table. Paradox cannot maintain the integrity of the key fields and at the same time change the order of the records. When you specify a table to hold the data, Paradox creates a table with the same structure as the source table, but without key fields.

Because the existence of several tables with the same records can compromise the integrity of your data, Paradox gives you another method of sorting keyed tables: *secondary indexes*. When you create a secondary index, you can use it to temporarily sort a keyed table by criteria other than the specified keys.

There are three ways to create secondary indexes: two are based on a single field, and a third allows secondary indexes to be based on several fields. To use either of the first two, the table must be on the desktop.

Say you want to be able to view your records sorted by Company, instead of by the person's name. Choose Window Close All to clear the desktop, and follow these Quick Steps.

Creating a Secondary Index

1. Choose File Utilities Restructure.

2. Select the table for which you want a secondary index (in this example ROLOTEMP.DB), then select OK.

3. In the Restructure dialog box, pull down the Table Properties list box and select Secondary Indexes.

4. Choose Define. The Define Secondary Index dialog box appears, as shown in Figure 5.14.

5. From the Fields list, select the field on which to create the index (in this example, Company) and click the right arrow.

6. Choose OK.

7. Type a name to save the index as, then select OK.

Paradox saves the secondary index.

8. Choose Save to return to the table.

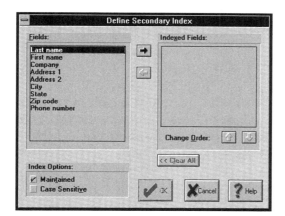

Figure 5.14
The Define Secondary Index dialog box.

To choose a secondary index, choose Table Order/Range. You'll see the Order/Range dialog box shown in Figure 5.15. As you can see, you now have a choice of two indexes:

*Last name-First name

Company

Note that the first of these indexes—the one you established using key fields—is marked by an asterisk.

TIP: To restructure a table that's already on the desktop, you don't have to close it first. Just select the table you want to restructure and use the Table Restructure command instead of **F**ile **U**tilities Restructure.

Figure 5.15
The Order / Range dialog box.

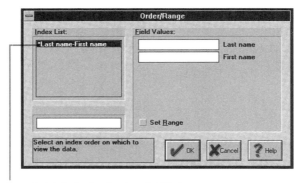

An asterisk indicates the key field index.

You can establish multiple-field secondary indexes just as easily as single-field indexes—and as many as you want. Then, whenever you want to change the apparent order of your data, you can use the Table Order/Range command to choose the appropriate index. This allows you to view your data in many ways without creating extraneous tables.

Points to Ponder

In this example, you were able to salvage the one record that violated the key criteria by adding some extra data—a middle initial. It's easy to do this in an arbitrary example. But what if the person in your offending record didn't have a middle initial, or you didn't know what it was? You would have to find another way to "key" the data.

In Chapter 6, you'll learn a great deal more about restructuring tables, and you'll learn how to deal with the problems raised here. For now, use the File Utilities Delete command to delete the ROLOTEMP and JONESES tables because you won't be needing them anymore. Next, we'll consider more efficient ways to use key fields, among other issues.

Move a Field in a Field Roster

1. Click on the field number in the first column of the field to move.
2. Click again, and drag the row to the new location.

Change an Item's Properties

1. Right-click on the item whose properties should be changed

   or

   Select the item whose properties should be changed and choose Properties. Choose the item to be changed from the menu.
2. Choose the aspect of the object to be changed from the submenu.
3. Choose a setting from the next submenu.
4. To save the changes, choose Properties View Properties Save.

Define a Picture

1. Choose File Utilities Restructure if the table is not on the desktop, or Table Restructure if it is.
2. Choose Assist.
3. Enter the picture in the Picture field.
4. Enter sample data in the Sample Picture field.
5. Choose Test Picture.
6. Choose Add to list.
7. Describe the picture, select OK.
8. Choose OK.

6

Modifying and Fine-Tuning Tables

In Chapter 5, you used the File Utilities Restructure command to add key fields to a table. But there's more you can do with this command, and there are other ways to change the appearance of your tables. In this chapter, you'll examine these techniques. In the process, you'll learn quite a bit more about key fields.

More About Restructuring

In Chapter 5, you added two key fields to a version of the ROLODEX table. As you learned, this resulted in key violations—several records whose key fields contained the same data. It was suggested in that chapter that the ideal set of key fields for the ROLODEX table would be Last name, First name, and Phone number.

However, Paradox requires that all key fields in a table appear in the structure before any non-key fields. At present, the Phone number field is the last field in the Field Roster. Fortunately, Paradox also provides an easy way around this problem, but it has consequences.

Moving a Field

The first step is to set your key fields:

- Last name
- First name
- Phone number

Choose File Utilities Restructure again, and select the ROLODEX table. As you may remember, you make a field a key field by pressing a key or double-clicking when its Key column in the Field Roster is highlighted, placing an asterisk in the column. Place the asterisks in the appropriate records. Choose Save to save your work, and you'll see, as you should expect, the message:

```
Key fields must be consecutive; starting with the first
field in the Field Roster.
```

This means that there are nonkey fields between the Phone number field and the other key fields. What to do? Obviously, you have to move the Phone number field. To do so, follow these Quick Steps.

Moving a Field
in a Field Roster

1. Click on the field number in the first column of the row representing the field to move.

Paradox highlights the field number.

2. Click again, and drag the row to the point where you want it to appear.

As you drag, a box will form around the field, and the pointer will turn into a two-headed arrow, as shown in Figure 6.1.

3. When the row is in its desired position, release the mouse button.

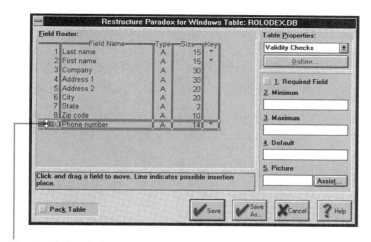

Figure 6.1
Moving a field in a Field Roster.

The double-headed arrow appears, to let you know you're dragging the field.

Choose Save to save your work, and you're done. The ROLODEX table will appear in your desktop, with one significant change: the Phone number field now appears next to the First name field, as shown in Figure 6.2, and you don't want it there. Later in this chapter, you'll find out what to do about that.

Adding a Field to a Table

In Chapter 5, I suggested that one way to deal with multiple records containing similar information is to create an arbitrary key field. This technique is appropriate for the Customer database, where it's quite likely that you'll have several records with the same names, so you'll add such a field. Later in the chapter, you'll use the same techniques to add a memo field—a data type you haven't used before—to the ROLODEX table. In Chapter 8, you'll learn how to use that field.

Figure 6.2
The result of moving a field.

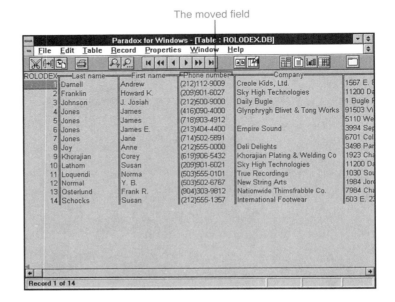

The moved field

QUICK STEPS

Adding a Field to a Table

1. Choose Window Close All.   Paradox clears the desktop.

2. Choose File Utilities Restructure again, and select the CUSTOMER table.   Paradox displays the Field Roster.

3. Key fields must appear before non-key fields. Since you have no key fields yet and the cursor is in the first record, press Ins.   Paradox creates space for the key field.

4. Type the data for the new record. (In this case, type the following data:
`Cust. ID A 5 *.)`

Your screen should now look like Figure 6.3.

5. Choose Save.

Paradox restructures the table so that it is sorted according to the key field.

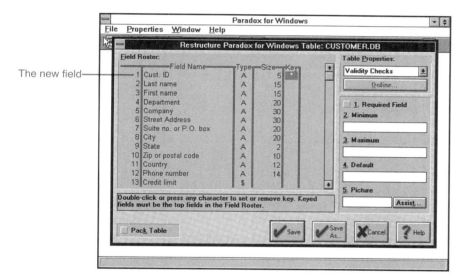

The new field

Figure 6.3
Adding a field to a table.

NOTE: As with editing a table, you can delete a record from the Field Roster—and the resulting database—by selecting the field and pressing Ctrl + Del. When you choose Save, you'll be asked to confirm that you really want to delete the field.

Now you have a problem. You've added a key field. The key field is blank in both of your records, so you've got a key violation, as you can see in Figure 6.4. (The windows have been rearranged so you can see what's going on. You may want to do the same.)

Figure 6.4

The result of adding a key field.

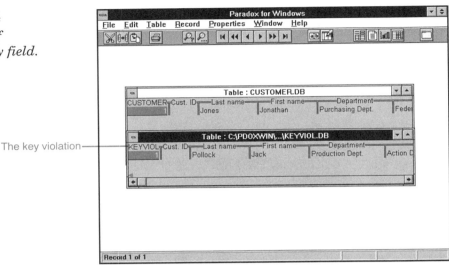

However, as I've suggested, this field should contain an arbitrary value. The simplest way to assign a unique identifier to each field is to use consecutive five-digit numbers. Press F9 to edit the KEYVIOL table. Press Tab ↹ and type 00001 in the Cust. ID field. Press F9 when you're done.

Now select the CUSTOMER table. Press F9 to go into Edit mode; then press Tab ↹ to move to the Cust. ID field and type 00002. Press F9 once more.

Now choose File Utilities Add to add the record in the KEYVIOL table to the CUSTOMER table as explained in Chapter 5. (It won't matter at this point whether you pick Append, Update, or Append and Update. Don't check either of the view boxes, or you'll get a second copy of the table.) When you're done, both records will be in the CUSTOMER table, sorted by the arbitrary key field.

Changing a Field's Characteristics

You can change any field's characteristics by choosing File Utilities Restructure to display the Field Roster, and altering the values in the Field Type column. The most likely reason to do so is that you've made a field too narrow.

Making a Field Wider

In the Phone number field of the CUSTOMER table, for example (in both tables), you don't have room to enter an extension number. This could become a problem in dealing with companies that use a central switchboard number. You can widen that field.

> **TIP:** Unlike the File Utilities Restructure command, the Table Restructure command can work on tables that are on the desktop, because it automatically puts them away first.

Open the CUSTOMER table Field Roster while the table is still on the screen. This time use the Table Restructure command. (You'll see that the Phone number field is an Alphanumeric field of 14 characters. This leaves enough for an area code and phone number, with punctuation. You'll need space for an extension of up to four digits, plus something to identify the remaining characters as an extension.)

Your field should be able to hold a phone number that looks like (313)555-6009, x.3456, so you'll need room for eight more characters. Move your cursor to the Field Size column of the Phone number record, type 22 (for the number of spaces), and press ⏎Enter. Then select Save. Later in this chapter, I'll show you how to set up that field so that any phone numbers entered into it conform to the desired format.

(You might want to do something similar to the ROLODEX table. You might also want to widen the Company field by a character or two. If you remember, one of the company names was one character too long to fit.)

Making a Field Narrower

You can make a field smaller. You might want to do this if your table is becoming large and you want to conserve disk space. If you make a field smaller than the largest value it already contains, you'll have problems. To see the effects of such a change, clear the desktop, choose File Utilities Restructure and select the ROLODEX table again. Reduce the width of the Company field from 30 to 25. When you choose Save, you'll see the dialog/warning box shown in Figure 6.5, letting you know that you'll lose data, and giving you several options for dealing with the consequences:

- *Trim All Fields* truncates the values in any reduced field to fit into the new field size.

- *Trim No Fields* places all the records with fields that don't fit into a separate, temporary table called PROBLEMS. If you choose this option, you can then edit the records in the PROBLEMS table, using, say, more abbreviations, and then reinsert them into the source table with the File Utilities Add command.

- *Specify Trimming for Each Field* presents the dialog box and set of options you're looking at once for each field that may be truncated, and lets you decide which course to take for each.

- *The Cancel button* returns you to restructuring, so you can make further changes, or cancels the restructuring.

For now, choose Cancel, and choose Cancel again in the Restructure window to cancel the changes.

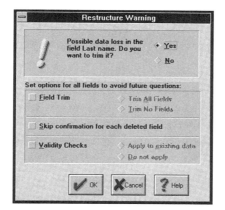

Figure 6.5
*Ways to deal with
truncated fields.*

Changing a Table's Properties

Whether or not you change the structure of a table, you can adjust the way it appears on the desktop—that is, modify its properties. You might want two particular fields next to each other so you can see the values in both of them at once. Or you may wish that your field displays were narrower so you could see more of a table at one time. You can also change many other aspects of the table's appearance.

Reordering the Display of Fields

Now you'll learn to move fields in a table window without affecting the actual table. Start with the ROLODEX table.

The Phone number field is in the wrong place, as you saw in Figure 6.2. It belongs at the end of the table, but because you made it into a key field, it is now in the third column. The easiest way to move it is with the Rotate key, Ctrl + R. Move the cursor to the Phone number field and press Ctrl + R.

Immediately, the third field changes to Company—just as it was in the original table. If you move right through the fields, you'll see that it's still followed by the Address 1 field, as it should be.

Where has the Phone number field gone? Press Esc to move to the last column in the table. You'll see that it's now the Phone number field. When you rotate fields, you move the current field to the end of the table, and move all the intervening fields one column to the left.

If you return the cursor to the third column and press Ctrl + R six more times, the Phone number field will appear in its old position, because you're rotating six columns. Press Ctrl + R a seventh time, and the Phone number field moves back to the end of the table window.

Now that you've seen that the view of a table on the desktop need not match its structure, you might contemplate other changes. Consider the effects of key fields on sorting order.

When a table has key fields, Paradox sorts it according to the key fields. If it has more than one key field, Paradox sorts the database using the values in all the key fields, taken together. The order in which the key fields appear in the Field Roster determines their order of precedence in sorting.

Thus, two people with the same last name will be sorted by their first names. Two people with the same first and last names will now be sorted by phone number (not by address, as they were before you added key fields). But that's not necessarily the most comfortable order in which to view the table or to enter data into it.

You might, for example, prefer to have the First name field shown first, followed by the Last name field. You can make this change with the Rotate key, Ctrl + R, as well. First, you'll rotate the First name field, and it will end up at the far end of the table. Then you must move to the second column, and rotate that column until the Last name field reappears.

TIP: Another way to move a column is to drag the heading to the desired location. This works as long as both the column to move and its target location are visible. If they aren't, you may be able to complete the move in two or more steps.

The changes you've made are considered changes to the table's *properties,* not to the table itself. Moreover, they are not permanent. They will disappear when you close the table unless you save them. To save them, choose Properties View Properties Save.

TIP: When you close a table whose properties have changed, Paradox always warns you of the fact and gives you a chance to save the changes. Choose Yes to make the changes permanent. They are saved in a separate file which is part of the table's family. If you want to save only some of the changes you've made to properties, choose Properties View Properties Save after making the ones you want to keep, but before making any others.

Changing Displayed Column Width

Suppose you want to see more of your ROLODEX table than will fit on the screen, even if its window is maximized. You can make any column narrower by moving the mouse pointer to the double-bar at its right, just below the column headers, and dragging to the left. You can move through the entire table and reduce the right margins of almost every column. The results appear in Figure 6.6.

Figure 6.6

Increasing the amount of data visible.

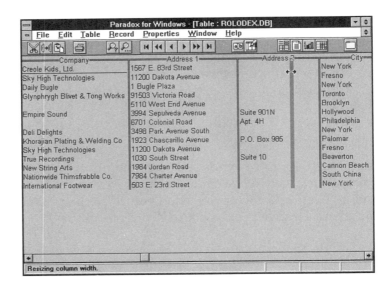

Once you've reduced a column, you can expand it again by dragging to the right. However, if it's an Alphanumeric field, you can expand it only up to its width as defined in the Field Roster.

Changing the Displayed Height of Your Records

You may have noticed that the leftmost visible field of the first visible record is always underscored. (You can see the underscore under Creole Kids, Ltd. in Figure 6.6.) You can use this line to change the height of your fields. Place the mouse pointer on it, and it becomes a two-headed arrow. You can then click and drag up or down to change the displayed height of your records. Doing so affects every record in the table. You may find this helpful if you want to use a font larger than the default. You'll also find it helpful to increase the height of records in this manner if you add graphics to a table, as described in Chapter 7.

Using the Properties Menus

As noted, you can change many aspects of a table's appearance. The place to start is at the Properties menu, shown in Figure 6.7. As you can see, you can make changes to the grid (the borders above and between columns), to the headings, and to the data. Each of these commands brings up a series of submenus, as indicated in Table 6.1. You can see these submenus by right-clicking on the appropriate object as well. Thus, for example, to see the properties menu for the Company field, you can either select the field and choose Properties Heading or right-click in the Company field (or select the field and use the shortcut key, Ctrl+H).

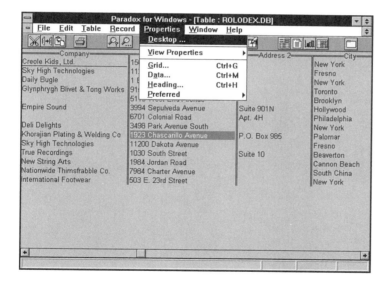

Figure 6.7
The Table Properties menu.

	Properties menu	Submenus	Sub-submenus	Choices or Sub-Sub-submenus
Table 6.1 *Table Properties That Can Be Changed*	Grid Properties	Color	Palette	
		Grid Lines	Heading Lines	
			Column Lines	
			Row Lines	
			Line Style	Style
			Color	Palette
			Spacing	Single
				Double
				Triple
		Current Record Marker	Show	
			Line Style	
			Color	Palette
	Data Properties	Data Dependent	(Choose range)	See Figure 6.8
		Alignment	Left	
			Center	
			Right	
			Top	
			Center	
			Bottom	
		Color	Palette	
		Font	Typeface	See Figure 6.9
			Size	See Figure 6.9
			Style	See Figure 6.9
			Color	Palette
	Heading Properties	Alignment	Left	
			Center	
			Right	
			Top	
			Center	
			Bottom	
		Color	Palette	
		Font	Typeface	See Figure 6.9
			Size	See Figure 6.9
			Style	See Figure 6.9
			Color	Palette

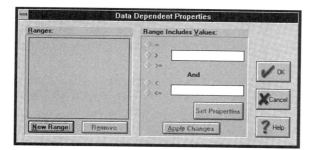

Figure 6.8
Specifying a range of values to which property changes should apply.

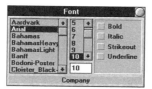

Figure 6.9
Specifying type characteristics.

TIP: Once you've "pinned" the Font dialog box to your desktop, it stays there until you close it by clicking on the thumbtack in the upper right corner. You can move from one part of the table to another and select fonts for each in turn.

Some elements of Table 6.1 require further explanation. When you choose Font, the submenu has a snap-shaped button at the top of it. If you choose Typeface, Size, or Style, you see a list of available options, from which you can select one. But if you click on the snap, the dialog box shown in Figure 6.9 appears. From there, you can choose all three. Close the dialog box by clicking on the snap. Anytime you choose Color, a palette of colors appears. The number of colors you can choose from depends on the way you have configured Windows. When you choose color at any point but a Font submenu, you select the background color for the object. If you choose Color from a Font submenu, you choose the color of the text.

If you choose Properties Data Data Dependent, you see the dialog box shown in Figure 6.8. Here you can specify certain values or ranges of values to which the properties you select should apply. This can be useful for highlighting such things as customers with the largest purchases, over-limit credit balances, specific states, and such. Of course, Paradox gives you many ways to select just those items, but it doesn't hurt to give yourself visual cues when you're perusing a table.

You can select properties for all the data in the table, or all the headings, by holding down the ⇧Shift key while pressing the shortcut keys. The menus are the same, but the results are applied to every column.

If you're not careful, you can get some pretty horrendous results, as Figure 6.10 shows. But you don't have to save the changes, and it's fun to fool around with while the boss isn't looking.

Figure 6.10

Applying properties with reckless disregard for principles of good design and taste.

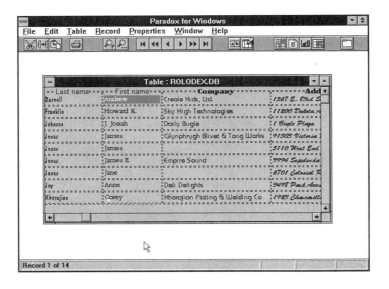

Changing an Item's Properties

1. Right-click on the item whose properties should be changed, or select the item whose properties should be changed and choose Properties.

Paradox displays a menu, the contents of which depend upon how you displayed the menu and which object is selected. Choose the item to be changed from the menu.

2. Choose the aspect of the object to be changed from the submenu.

3. Choose a setting from the next submenu.

Paradox closes the menu and applies the changes to the object.

4. To save the changes, choose Properties View Properties Save.

Controlling What Appears in a Field

There are many circumstances under which you'd want to control the contents of a field. When you set up controls of this type, you ensure that any new data entered into the field conforms to the format you establish.

There are two different ways to impose such controls:

- When you select a Numeric, Currency, or Date field, you can use the Properties menu (or the Object Inspector) to select from among several formats. You learned how to do that in Chapter 4.

- When you create or modify a table structure, you can impose *validity checks* on a field.

A validity check may restrict entries to a certain range, supply a default value, or assign a picture to a field. A picture (sometimes called an *edit mask*) defines exactly what types of characters can appear in a field, and automatically fills in any required characters. You'll learn how to create them now.

Validity Checking: Formatting Alphanumeric Fields

You control the appearance of Alphanumeric (and sometimes Numeric fields) by supplying *pictures* for them. You'll add some pictures to the CUSTOMER table. Choose Table Restructure to bring up the Restructure window. (If the CUSTOMER table isn't still on the desktop, use the File Utilities Restructure command instead.) We'll now use the area to the right of the Field Roster, which up to now we've studiously ignored.

In this area are several fields which allow you to define various types of validity checks. You can enter pictures directly in field number 5, but you'll find it much easier to create pictures if you choose Assist.

Pictures contain three types of elements:

- *Constant characters* are displayed literally.

- *Variables* restrict entries to any character of a given type.

- *Command characters* tell Paradox how to treat the other characters.

There are five command characters and five variable characters for pictures; they are summarized in Table 6.2. Any characters used in a picture (other than those in the table) are placed in the field automatically.

Character	Meaning
Command Characters	
[]	Items in brackets are optional elements.
,	Separates groups of acceptable alternatives.
*n	Allows entry of up to n characters of the specified type. If *n* is not specified, the number of characters may vary from none to the maximum the field will hold.
;	Indicates that the following character is to be entered literally if it would otherwise be a command character or a variable.
{}	Groups sets of characters to be separated by a comma.
Variable Characters	
#	Only numeric characters are accepted.
?	Only alphabetic characters are accepted.
&	Only alphabetic characters are accepted. The entered character is converted to uppercase.
@	Any character is accepted.
!	Any character is accepted. If alphabetic, the entered character is converted to uppercase.

Table 6.2
Picture Command and Variable Characters

Now let's experiment with a picture. Select the Phone number field. Recall that you wanted phone numbers to appear in the format:

```
(313)555-6009, x.3456
```

Follow these steps:

1. Choose Assist. You'll see the Picture Assistance dialog box shown in Figure 6.11.

2. In the Picture field, type the following value:

```
(###)###-####[;, x.####]
```

3. In the Sample Value field, type the phone number:

```
(503)333-2222.
```

4. Choose Test Value. The message area at the bottom of the dialog box will display either `Value is valid` or `Picture does not accept value`.

If you see the latter message, either you didn't type the picture correctly or you didn't type the phone number correctly.

TIP: To make sure you didn't use any of the picture characters incorrectly, choose Verify Syntax. This will not tell you if the picture correctly represents the value you want it to represent, only if you made a mistake in the way you used the picture characters.

Figure 6.11

The Picture Assistance dialog box.

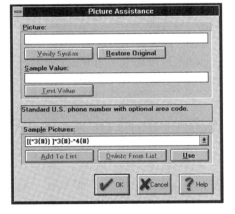

However, the picture isn't perfect yet. Try entering a number such as `(503)333-2222, x.34`.

If you type, say, a two-digit extension and then Test Value, Paradox displays the message `Value is valid so far, but may not be complete`. You'll fix the picture shortly.

As you can see, the picture you created includes two of the command characters: the brackets for the optional extension, and the semicolon to let Paradox know that the comma, a command character, is to be entered literally. The problem is that the picture contains the prefix for the extension (the comma, space, and so on), but will only accept exactly four numeric characters.

The variable will have to be a bit more complex. Move back to the Picture field. Edit the picture so that it reads:

```
(###)###-####[;, x.##[#][#]].
```

Granted, it's ugly, but it works. Here's how:

Paradox treats everything enclosed within a set of brackets as a unit. Within the brackets defining the optional extension, each of the two numeric character placeholders is enclosed in an extra set of brackets. This means that if you enter an extension, Paradox will supply the characters , x. and expect two digits. You can now optionally enter three or four, instead of two. If you had enclosed the two optional characters in only one extra set of brackets, such as [;, x.##[##]], Paradox would gladly accept two characters; but if you entered a third, it would insist on a fourth. While you're in this picture, you might want to add a set of brackets around the area code picture, so that the result looks like this:

```
[(###)]###-####[;, x.##[#][#]].
```

This will make the area code optional, so that you don't have to include it in local numbers. Then you can use the database for direct dialing, if you have a program that lets you do that. Test the value, and if everything works, choose OK.

Here's an easier example. Select the State field. Choose Assist, and type the picture && in the Picture field.

Now, when you enter a State abbreviation in lowercase, it will automatically appear in uppercase. (Try it in the Sample Value field and choose Test Value. If you enter anything other than a letter, Paradox will refuse to accept it. Choose OK when you're done.)

You can also provide alternatives. Select the Zip code field. The picture you'll create will accept either a Zip code of five or nine digits, or a British Commonwealth postal code. If you review Table 6.2, you'll see that you can provide alternatives by enclosing them in brackets and separating them with a comma. Choose Assist and enter this picture:

```
{#####[-####],&#& #&#}.
```

The first part of this picture, before the comma, is the Zip code. Note that the last four digits are optional because of the brackets, but the hyphen is supplied automatically if you go past the first five digits.

If you start your entry with a number, Paradox will expect a Zip code, because the only alternative starts with a letter. Conversely, if you start with a letter, you will be forced to enter a British Commonwealth postal code. Try out a few entries, and you'll see that this is true. Remember, you can clear a field with ⬅Backspace.

Pictures are limited, in that they have no effect on data already entered into the table. Indeed, all validity checks occur only when you press a key that moves the cursor out of the field to which the validity checks apply.

You might think that this means that Paradox can change existing entries that don't conform to your pictures. In fact, that's not true. Follow these Quick Steps to define a picture.

Defining a Picture

1. Choose File Utilities Restructure if the table is not on the desktop, or Table Restructure if it is.

2. Choose Assist.   Paradox displays the Picture Assistance dialog box.

3. Enter the picture in the **P**icture field.

4. Enter sample data in the **S**ample Picture field.

5. Choose Verify Syntax.   Paradox tells you `The pic-ture is correct`, whether it is or not.

6. Enter a sample value in the **S**ample Value field.

7. Choose Test Value.   Paradox either (a) responds with `Value is valid`, (b) responds with `Picture does not accept value` or (c) truncates your sample value and responds with `Value is valid`.

8. When you suspect that everything is working as you want it to, choose OK.

Other Types of Validity Checks

The Restructure and Create windows allow you to create several other types of validity checks. As you might guess from their command names, you can set a minimum value for a field with 2. Minimum, a maximum with 3. Maximum, or a default entry with 4. Default.

If your company never extends more than $25,000 of credit to any customer, for example, you might enter `25000` as the maximum acceptable value for the Credit limit field. Paradox would then refuse to accept any entries greater than that amount.

Another useful validity check is the Required Field check box. If you check this item, the field may not be left blank. You can use **R**equired in combination with other validity checks. Thus, you might use the picture ##### along with the **R**equired status in the Cust. ID field. You might want to make all fields **R**equired except some parts of the address.

NOTE: Think carefully before selecting **R**equired fields. If there were **R**equired fields for which some customers could offer no appropriate values, such as Department or Suite no., your clerks would be unable to process their orders.

As a final step, let's add several new fields of different types to the ROLODEX table. You'll learn what to do with them in Chapter 7. Follow these steps:

1. Choose **File Utilities Restructure** command, and select the ROLODEX table.

2. Press PgDn to move to the last row.

3. Press ↓ to create a new record.

4. Enter the values `Notes M 30`.

5. Press ↓ to create a new record.

6. Enter the values `Formatted F 30`.

7. Press ↓ to create a new record.

8. Enter the values `Illustration G`.

9. Choose Save.

When the ROLODEX table appears on the desktop, press End), and you'll see that, sure enough, the three new fields have been added to the right-hand end of the table.

Creating or Editing a Memo Field

1. Make the field current.
2. Press F9 or click the Edit button on the speedbar.
3. Press F2 or click the Field View button on the speedbar.
4. Enter or edit the text as you would in any Windows application.
5. Double-click the close box when you are finished or press F2 again.

Search and Replace

1. Make sure the cursor is placed above or before the first instance of the text to be replaced.
2. Select Edit Search Text.
3. Enter the text to search for and the text with which to replace it.
4. Press Alt + S or click Search.
5. To replace the text, press Alt + R or click Replace. To skip it and search for the next instance, press Alt + S or click Search.

Paste Data into a Database Via the Clipboard

1. Make a Memo, Formatted Memo, or Graphic field current.
2. Press F2 or click the Field View button.
3. Open the source file in the application with which it was created, and choose Edit Copy to copy to the Clipboard the part you want to use.
4. Return to Paradox and choose Edit Paste or click the Paste icon on the speedbar.

Working with Embedded Objects

In Chapter 6, you added Memo, Formatted Memo, and Graphic fields to your ROLODEX table. In this chapter you'll learn what you can do with them.

What Is a BLOB?

BLOB is short for *Binary Large OBject*. This refers to any type of data that is linked to your table file, but not stored in it. Memos and formatted memos can be as large as the space available on your hard disk. However, since you specified a size of 30 for each of these fields, only 30 characters of these fields will appear in the table until you go into Field view.

When you have BLOBs in your file, all that Paradox actually stores in your database table is some information about the location of the file containing the BLOB, and the location of the BLOB in the file. When you have entered data in a Memo or a Formatted memo field and make the field visible on the desktop, the field will display its contents, up to the number of characters you specified in the field roster. In a Graphic field, all that appears is the text <BLOB Graphic>.

When you move to a record in a Formatted memo field that contains data, any formatting that you've added to the text appears in the space allotted for the field on the screen. When you leave that record, the text becomes unformatted again, appearing in the default font and style which you've selected for the field. Similarly, when you move into a Graphic field that contains data, the portion of the image that will fit in the available space appears on your screen.

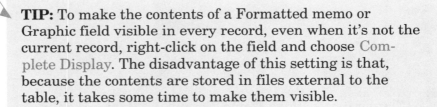

TIP: To make the contents of a Formatted memo or Graphic field visible in every record, even when it's not the current record, right-click on the field and choose Complete Display. The disadvantage of this setting is that, because the contents are stored in files external to the table, it takes some time to make them visible.

Placing Data in a BLOB Field

There are basically five ways to get data into a Memo or Formatted memo field:

- Use the **E**dit menu (shown in Figure 7.1) to insert the data from another file with the Paste **F**rom command.

- Move the cursor to the memo held, then press F2 or click the Field View button or double-click in the field to go into Field view, and enter the data from the keyboard.

- Use the **E**dit menu or the Paste icon to paste the data from the Clipboard with the **P**aste command.

- Use Object Linking and Embedding (OLE) to embed a "live" file in your table (a topic beyond the scope of this book).

- Use Dynamic Data Exchange (DDE) to link specific data in another file to a database field (another topic beyond the scope of this book).

You can use all but the first method to place data in a Graphic field.

Field View button

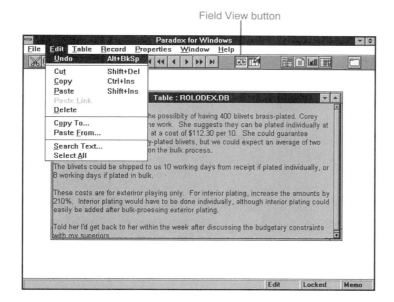

Figure 7.1
The Edit menu.

If you use **E**dit Paste **F**rom to paste from a file, you can paste a text file (.PXT, .TXT) or a Rich Text Format (.RTF) file into either a Memo or Formatted memo field. The difference is that when you paste a file into a Memo field, it becomes unformatted text; whereas when you paste a Rich Text file into a Formatted memo field, it retains its formatting. (Graphic fields are discussed later in this chapter.) Follow the Quick Steps below to complete the procedure. If you want to paste text from another type of file created by a Windows application, you can paste it into a Memo field by first cutting it to the Clipboard, then using the Paste command.

Inserting a File into a Memo or Formatted Memo Field

1. Press F9 or click the Edit Data button if you are not already in Edit mode.

Paradox puts the table in Edit mode.

2. Make the target field current.

3. Press F2 or click the Field View button on the speed-bar.

Paradox opens a memo window.

4. Choose Edit Paste From.

Paradox displays a File Browser, showing files of the appropriate type for the field.

5. If necessary, choose Browse to find the file you want.

6. Select the file to insert and click OK.

Paradox pastes the entire file into the Graphic field.

7. Double-click the close box or press ⇧Shift+F2 to leave Field view.

Pasting Data into a Memo or Formatted Memo Field via the Clipboard

1. Press F9 or click the Edit Data button if you are not already in Edit mode.

Paradox puts the table in Edit mode.

2. Make the target field current.

3. Press `F2` or click the Field View button.

Paradox opens a memo window.

4. Press `Alt`+`Tab⇄` repeatedly until you return to the Windows Program Manager, or press `Ctrl`+`Esc` to view the Task List and select Program Manager.

5. Open the application with which the file was created, and load the file you want to use.

6. Select the portion of the text you want to use and choose Edit Copy.

Windows copies the selected part to the Clipboard.

7. Return to Paradox and choose Edit Paste or click the Paste icon on the speedbar.

Paradox pastes the image from the Clipboard into the open field.

8. Double-click the close box or press `⇧Shift`+`F2` to leave Field view.

Entering Text in a Memo Field

Let's look at a Memo field now. Suppose you just placed an order for several hundred Standard Mark IV blivets from the Glynphrygh Blivet and Tong Works, and you want to have them brass-plated. You'll record the relevant details of your conversation with Ms. Khorajian in the Notes field. Move to the record for Corey Khorajian, and then move to your new Notes field. Go into Field view, and a window will open that completely covers the table window. You might enter text such as the following:

```
Called on July 24 to discuss the possibility of having
400 blivets brass-plated. Corey sees no problem in
handling the work. She suggests they can be plated
individually at a cost of $12.76 ea. or in bulk at a
cost of $112.30 per 10. She could guarantee first-
quality work on individually-plated blivets, but we
could expect an average of two minor blemishes per lot
of 10 on the bulk process.

The blivets could be shipped to us 10 working days from
receipt if plated individually, or 8 working days if
plated in bulk.

These costs are for exterior plating only. For interior
plating, increase the amounts by 210%. Interior plating
would have to be done individually, although interior
plating could easily be added after bulk-processing
exterior plating.

Told her I'd get back to her within the week after
discussing the budgetary constraints with my superiors.
```

If you've ever used the Windows Notepad, you know how to enter text in a Memo field. All the methods of entering and editing text are substantially the same as those used in the Notepad. As you probably know, you don't press ⏎Enter until you reach the end of a paragraph; the text will "wrap" as it reaches the right border of the window (see Figure 7.2). If you change the size of the window, the text will adjust itself accordingly, as shown in Figure 7.3. The only difference is in the search-and-replace feature, which I will discuss shortly.

When you're through entering text in a Memo or Formatted memo field, press F2 again, or double-click the close box, or click the Field View icon, and you'll return to your table. Your memo will be saved automatically.

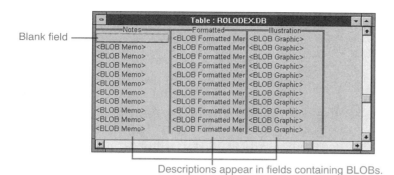

Blank field

Descriptions appear in fields containing BLOBs.

Figure 7.2
Text in a Memo field.

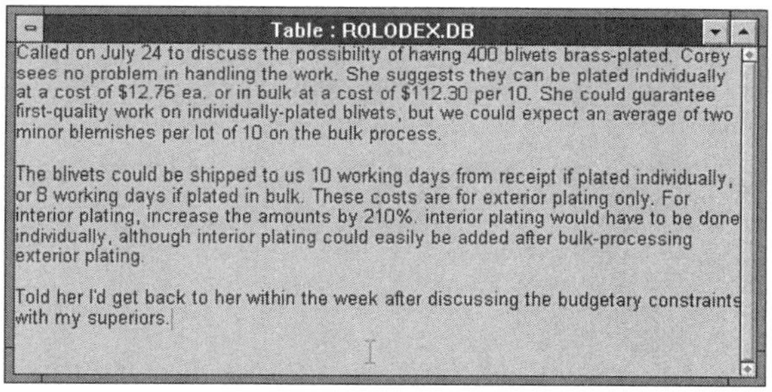

Figure 7.3
A maximized Memo field.

Browsing Through Memos

To view the contents of a Memo field from Main mode, you enter Field view, just as you do while editing. You'll be back in the editing window, but you won't be able to make any changes. If you look at the status bar, you'll see that the Field indicator is present, but the Edit indicator isn't.

Working with Blocks of Text

To edit more than a few characters in a Memo field, you should use block operations. These involve selecting text, either with the keyboard or with the mouse, and using the commands on the **E**dit menu or their speedbar shortcuts (see Figure 7.4).

To understand block operations, you must be clear on the difference between cutting, copying, and deleting. When you delete text, you can't get it back; it is gone forever. When you cut text, you move it to a special Windows accessory called the Clipboard. When you copy text, it remains in your file, but appears on the Clipboard as well. Any text on the Clipboard can be pasted into your memo. The Clipboard thus functions as a holding area for text as you move it around in your Memo field.

> **TIP:** You can also use the **E**dit menu commands, their equivalent speedbar buttons, and the Clipboard to cut, copy, and paste data among other types of fields, so long as the data is appropriate to the field type.

These procedures work the same way as they do in all other Windows applications. If you're not familiar with using the Clipboard and its associated commands, see your Windows documentation.

> **TIP:** Whatever you cut or copy to the Clipboard remains there until you cut or copy something else or until you exit Windows. This means that you can use the Clipboard to create boilerplate text, which you can insert into any Memo field in any table.

If you were to choose Complete Display in the Object Inspector and widen the Notes field a bit, your title would appear as shown in Figure 7.4.

Close the window, and we'll explore a few more Editor features.

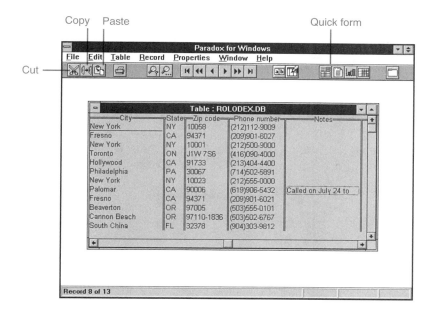

Figure 7.4
The visible portion of a Memo field.

Searching and Replacing

As noted, Paradox has its own Search feature, which is somewhat different from that of the Notepad. Choose Edit Search Text to open the Search & Replace dialog box (see Figure 7.5).

The Replace feature lets you search through the entire memo, finding each instance of the text for which you're looking. At each one, you can decide whether to replace it or leave it alone and go on to the next one. Alternatively, you can replace every instance or just stop when you've found the one you want.

Try this feature now:

1. Select your filled-in Notes field and go into Field view. Make sure you're still in Edit mode.

2. Choose Edit Search Text.

3. Enter the text to search for (`blivet`) in the Search **F**or box.

4. Enter the text to replace it with (`tong`) in the Replace **W**ith box.

5. Click Search. The first instance of blivet will be high-lighted. (You may have to move the dialog box to see the highlight in the window.)

6. If you want to replace the text, press Alt+R or click Replace. The word blivet is replaced by the word tong, and the next instance of blivet is highlighted. If you don't want to replace it, press Alt+S or click Search again instead. The highlight moves to the next instance of blivet, but the previous one is unchanged. Try one of each.

Figure 7.5
The Search &
Replace dialog box.

The following Quick Steps show you how to search for and replace text in a Memo field.

Searching and Replacing Memo Text

1. Open a memo window and make sure the cursor is placed above or before the first instance of the text to be replaced.

2. Select Edit Search Text.   Paradox presents the Search & Replace dialog box.

3. Enter the text to search for in the Search **F**or: field (in this example, `blivet`).

4. Enter the text with which to replace it in the Replace **W**ith field (in this example `tong`), and click Search.

Paradox highlights the first instance of the search text and displays the message `Match found` (see Figure 7.6).

5. To replace this instance, press `Alt`+`R` or click Replace. To skip it and search for the next instance, click Search.

If you choose **R**eplace, Paradox replaces the highlighted text and moves on to the next instance. If you choose **S**earch, Paradox highlights the next instance, without replacing the first. If there are no more instances, Paradox displays the message `"No Match found."`

6. To end the process, click Cancel.

NOTE: To replace only instances in which the case of the text you enter matches that in the file, first click the Case Sensitive check box. After Paradox for Windows finds the word you're searching for, you can choose Replace **A**ll to replace all occurrences of the original word with the new word.

When you're finished, repeat the procedure, replacing `tong` with `blivet`, to restore your original text.

Figure 7.6
Replacing text.

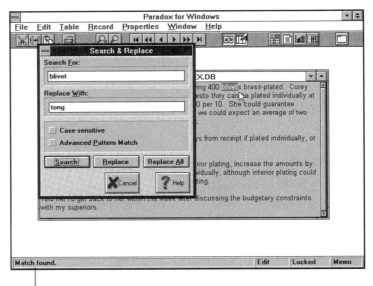

Paradox tells you when it finds a match.

Other Uses for Memo Fields

In this chapter, you've seen a Memo field used to add random notes to a list of names. You might want to use such a field for adding personal information, so that you remember to send regards to your contact's family members by name, for example.

Similarly, you might use a Memo field to store information about a person's specific accomplishments in a personnel directory table. If a proposal you're submitting includes a list of the people who will be working on the project, you can then enhance that list with details about the relevant skills of each member of the team.

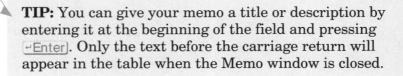

TIP: You can give your memo a title or description by entering it at the beginning of the field and pressing ⤶Enter. Only the text before the carriage return will appear in the table when the Memo window is closed.

Formatting Memo Fields

Formatted memo fields are just like Memo fields, except that you have access to all the text-styling features built into Windows. You can change the font, size, color, and style of any text you first select by right-clicking on the selection to display the object inspector. These text attributes will be saved along with the memo. Figure 7.7 shows a Formatted memo field.

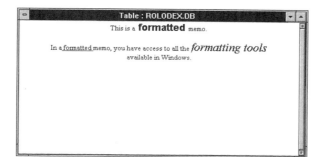

Figure 7.7

A Formatted memo field.

Uses for Formatted Memo and Graphic Fields

One advantage of the Windows environment is that every application shares the same means of formatting text—adding color, setting fonts, and adding styling such as boldfacing and underlining. This is part of what makes it possible for applications to share data. For this reason, Formatted memo fields are an excellent way of linking complete documents to a Paradox database. If you first save the document in Rich Text format, all the formatting will be preserved when you read it into your database. (Rich Text format files are indicated by an .RTF extension; this format is available to you in many Windows applications.)

There are many uses for Graphic fields in databases. A personnel database might include scanned photographs of every member of the staff for easy identification. With the

continues

continued

right equipment, the information stored in such a database could easily be used to produce photo identification cards.

An inventory database could include pictures—drawings or scanned photographs—of the items available. Such a database could then be used to produce illustrated catalogs.

Using Graphic Fields

To use a Graphic field, you simply paste a graphic image into it. Use either of the Quick Steps below to complete the operation. Paradox will accept these files: Paintbrush (.PCX), Windows Bitmap (.BMP), TIFF (.TIF), and Encapsulated PostScript (.EPS). If you want to try the feature, and you don't have any appropriate files, set your screen up in an attractive manner, and then press PrtSc to copy your entire screen to the Clipboard. Go into Edit mode (F9 or click the Edit Data Speedbar tool). Next, select the Illustration field in one of the records, and choose Edit Paste.

Windows will paste the image on the Clipboard into your file. To view it, go into Field view. You'll see something like Figure 7.8. If you want to see more of the image, maximize the window or use the scroll bars.

Pasting a Graphic Image via the Clipboard

1. Press F9 or click the Edit Data button if you are not already in Edit mode.	Paradox puts the table into Edit mode.
2. Make a Graphic field current.	

3. Press F2 or click the Field View button.

Paradox opens a Graphic window.

4. Press Alt+Tab⇥ repeatedly until you return to the Windows Program Manager.

5. Open a graphics application and load the file you want to use.

6. Select the portion of the image you want to use and choose Edit Copy.

Windows copies the selected part to the Clipboard.

7. Return to Paradox and choose Edit Paste or click the Paste icon on the speedbar.

Paradox pastes the image from the Clipboard into the Graphic field.

8. Double-click the close box or press ⇧Shift+F2 to leave Field view.

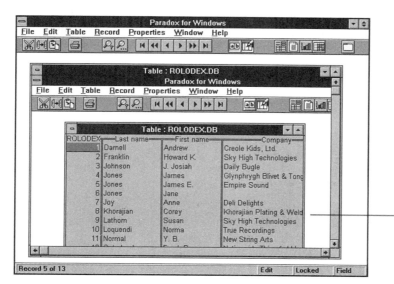

Figure 7.8
Viewing an image in a Graphic field.

A snapshot of your screen

**Pasting a Graphic File
into a Database**

1. Press F9 or click the Edit Data button if you are not in Edit mode.

   Paradox puts the table in Edit mode.

2. Make a Graphic field current.

3. Press F2 or click the Edit Data button.

   Paradox opens the Graphic window.

4. Press F2 or click the Field View button on the speedbar.

5. Choose Edit Paste From.

   Paradox displays a second file browser, with extensions matching the compatible graphic file types.

6. If necessary, choose Browse to find the file you want.

7. Select the file to insert and click OK.

   Paradox pastes the entire file into the Graphic field.

8. Double-click the close box or press ⇧Shift+F2 to leave Field view.

Embedded Objects in Forms

Paradox handles embedded objects very differently when you view your table in a form. Click the Quick Form button (see Figure 7.3) or choose File New Form. You'll see a new form with all the fields currently existing in your ROLODEX table. As you can see in Figure 7.9, Paradox reserves a reasonably large area for embedded objects in forms. If you go into Field view, instead of opening a separate window for Memo or Formatted memo fields, Paradox lets you move through the field in the allotted space using the cursor keys. You can't see more of a graphic image, but you can see the upper left corner, which should be enough to give you a hint of the field's contents.

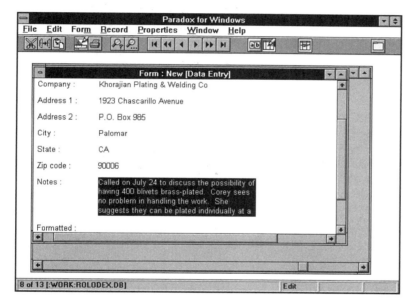

Figure 7.9
Viewing embedded objects in a form.

TIP: You can't adjust the size or position of a Graphic object in a form; however, you can adjust the portion of it that's shown (and that portion's size) in a table using the Object Inspector, as Figure 7.10 shows. And under some mysterious circumstances, you can get scroll bars on the graphic in a table, even without going into Field view. You can also adjust the height of the fields in a table, as explained in Chapter 6.

Figure 7.10

The Graphic field Object Inspector.

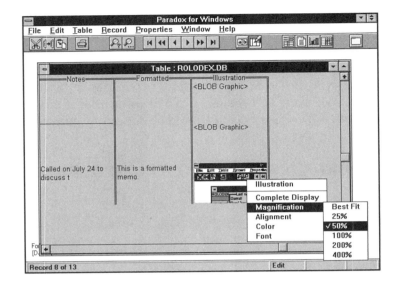

You probably don't have much use for formatted memos or illustrations in a Rolodex file, but these types of fields definitely have their uses. See the FYIdeas in this chapter for some examples. (If you plan to use the Rolodex file for your own purposes, you may want to restructure it to delete these last two fields. You'll probably find the notes file handy.)

Creating a Query Table

1. Choose File New Query.
2. Select the table about which to inquire and choose OK.
3. To inquire about more than one table, choose Query Add Table, select the table, and choose OK.
4. Place check marks in the check boxes of the fields to be included in the ANSWER table.
5. Place example elements in fields on which you wish to perform calculations, or you wish to link to fields in other tables in the query.
6. Enter any values to find, or calculations to perform.

Running a Query

1. Choose File New Query.
2. Select a table name from the list and choose OK.
3. Check the fields you want to see in your ANSWER table.
4. Enter the values for which you wish to search into the appropriate fields.
5. Press F8 or choose Query Run or click the Run Query icon.

Saving an ANSWER Table

1. Choose File Utilities Rename.
2. Choose the table :PRIV:ANSWER.DB.
3. Enter the New name for the table.
4. Choose Rename.

Printing the Contents of an ANSWER Table

1. Select the ANSWER table.
2. Press Shift + F7, or choose Table Quick Report, or click the Quick Report icon.

Getting Information from Your Database

The reason you create databases is to get information from the data you've stored in them. You get information from a database by viewing selected groups of items sharing some common characteristics. For example, you might want to see a list of all salespeople who sold at least $25,000 worth of goods in any month. Or you might want to compare January's sales with July's sales. You may be interested in which states generated the most orders, or which customers placed the largest orders.

These examples all suggest ways of selecting a group of *records* from your database. But you might also want to select *fields*. You might, for example, want a list of the names and phone numbers of all your customers, or a list of companies and their states and Zip codes for planning a mass mailing.

Further, you might want to limit your selections by both field and record. Having found that, say, your largest orders came from

Texas, you might want a list of the names and companies representing all your orders from that state.

In essence, then, you get information from your database by *searching* for various items, or by *querying* your data, as it's called. In this chapter, you'll learn many ways of using Paradox's sophisticated querying techniques to make changes to the data stored in your databases.

Creating a Query Table

The method of querying databases in Paradox is called *query by example (QBE)*, and it's extremely easy to use. You simply fill out a form telling Paradox the information that you want to look for, and Paradox finds it for you.

To begin a query, choose File New Query. Then, from the Select File dialog box, select the table from which you want information . When you do, Paradox opens a window in which you see what looks like an empty version of the table itself. All that's in the various fields is a check box. This is a *query window*, which can contain one or more *query tables*. You use these tables to select fields and values to display. When you have made your selections and processed the query, everything matching the criteria you have established appears in a separate, temporary table called ANSWER.

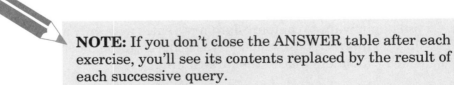

NOTE: If you don't close the ANSWER table after each exercise, you'll see its contents replaced by the result of each successive query.

Selecting Fields to Include in the ANSWER Table

The methods for selecting fields to include in the ANSWER table are different from those for selecting the values—or the records— to include. Start with fields.

Use your ROLODEX table as an example since it has enough information in it to make queries interesting. The following exercise will display just the two name fields in the ANSWER table. Follow these Quick Steps to create the query table.

Creating a Query Table

1. Choose **File New Query**.

or

If it is on the speedbar, right-click on the New Query icon and choose New.

2. Select the table about which you wish to inquire (in this case, ROLODEX), and choose OK.

Paradox creates a new query window, with a query table for the Rolodex file, as shown in Figure 8.1.

3. If you wish to inquire about more than one table (you won't in this exercise), choose Query Add Table.

or

continues

continued

Click the Add Query Table icon.	Paradox places the second query table in the query window.
4. Select the table and choose OK.	
5. Place check marks in the check boxes of the fields you want included in the ANSWER table.	Check marks appear.
6. Place example elements in fields in which you wish to perform calculations, or in which you wish to link to fields in other tables in the query.	
7. Enter any values to find, or calculations to perform.	

Paradox creates a new query window, with a query table for the Rolodex file, as you see in Figure 8.1. Its function, however, is clearly indicated by the title Query: <Untitled> in the window's top border.

As you can see in the figure, the menu and the speedbar change when you open a query window. You'll see explanations of the icons in Figure 8.1. You'll get to use some of the new ones in the course of this chapter and the next.

To include a field in a query, place a check mark in the field with the Check key, F6. You'll learn the functions of other keys later in the chapter.

Click the check box in the First name field, or press F6. You'll see a check mark appear in the box. Now do the same in the Last name field. You should see another check mark appear. Your query window should look like Figure 8.2. You have now selected two fields to include in your ANSWER table. Press F8, choose Query Run, or click the Run Query icon to process the query. A Query Status message box will inform you of Paradox's progress. The result should look like Figure 8.3.

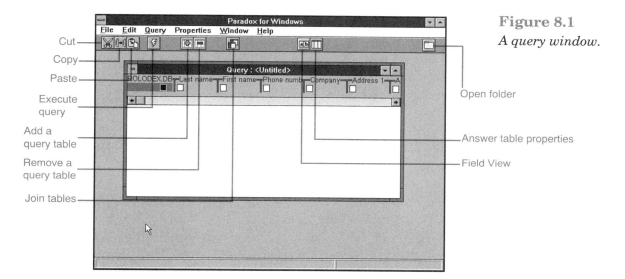

Cut
Copy
Paste
Execute query
Add a query table
Remove a query table
Join tables

Open folder
Answer table properties
Field View

Figure 8.1
A query window.

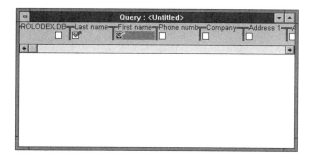

Figure 8.2
Selecting fields for a query.

Figure 8.3
Displaying selected fields.

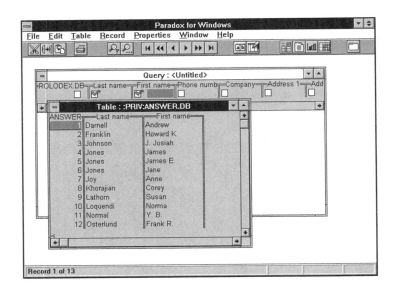

NOTE: I've moved and resized the ANSWER table so that you can see both the query and the result. I'll follow this procedure throughout this and the next two chapters. On your computer, the ANSWER table will be cascaded over the query window.

But there's something wrong here, isn't there? There were 14 records in the ROLODEX table, but only 13 appear in the AN-SWER table! What's missing? Notice that there's only one James Jones in the ANSWER table. In the ANSWER table, Paradox displays only those items that are unique. You may know that the two James Joneses are different people, but without the information from another field to differentiate them, Paradox doesn't.

Including All Records

Paradox is smart enough to realize that you may want to see all the records, regardless of whether or not they are unique. So it gives you a tool for doing so. Make the query window current. Choose one of the fields you selected with a check mark, and press ⇧Shift+F6. A plus sign is added to the check mark (this is the *Check Plus* mark). This tells Paradox to include all records, even duplicates, in that field. Press F8 or choose **Q**uery **R**un or its icon, and you should now see all your records, as illustrated in Figure 8.4.

TIP: Paradox has four kinds of check marks for indicating the way a field should be included in a query. There are two ways to enter these marks. With the keyboard, move to the desired field and press ⇧Shift+F6 until the desired mark appears. With the mouse, hold down the left button when the pointer is in the check box, and you'll see this menu of check marks:

Drag to the one you want to use and release the button. (The fourth mark, the *Group By* mark, is beyond the scope of this book.)

As you know, the order of the fields in a table window on the desktop may not be the same as that of the fields in the table on disk. The fields in the table file follow the order of the field names in the Field Roster, while you can rotate fields in a table window and save the changes as table properties. However, fields in ANSWER tables reflect the ordering imposed by the Field Roster (called *table order*), rather than that indicated by the query table (called *image order*). The records in the ANSWER table will be sorted in ascending order from left to right, just as if you had used the Table Sort command and chosen the leftmost field (as defined in the Field Roster) as the sort criterion.

Figure 8.4

*The effect of the
Check Plus key.*

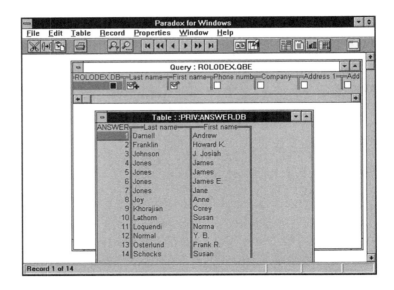

Sorting the ANSWER Table

Suppose you want a list of the people in your database sorted by
the company for which they work. Of course, you'll want the people
sorted by last name, in case you have several people who work for
the same company.

Place a check mark in the First name, Last name, and
Company fields. Next, choose Properties Answer Table Sort.
You'll see the Sort Answer dialog box shown in Figure 8.5. You use
this the same way as you do a standard sorting dialog box, except
that you can't choose to sort in descending order. Set it up as
shown, and choose OK. Then run the query by pressing F8,
clicking the Run Query icon, or choosing Query Run. You'll see the
result in Figure 8.6. Later in this chapter, I'll show you how to
exclude the record that doesn't contain a company name.

NOTE: You can rearrange the order of the fields in the
query table, but it won't affect the ANSWER table.
However, once you've gotten an ANSWER table, you can
rearrange or sort it as you would any other table.

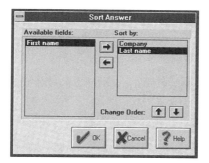

Figure 8.5
The Sort Answer dialog box.

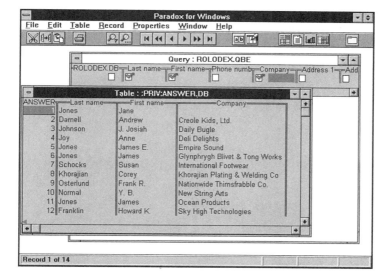

Figure 8.6
The result of sorting the ANSWER table.

Sorting in Reverse Order

A query can sort your records in reverse order if you wish. To do so, use the *Check Descending* mark, a check mark followed by a down arrow (see Figure 8.7). Then select the fields to be sorted using the Properties Answer Table Sort command.

To produce an ANSWER table with the companies sorted in reverse order, follow these steps:

1. Select the query window.

2. Move to the Company field and press ⇧Shift + F6 twice, until you see the Check Descending mark.

3. Choose Properties Answer Table Sort.

4. If your Sort Answer dialog box doesn't look like Figure 8.5, select Company and click →.

5. Select Last name and click →.

6. Choose OK.

7. Run the query. You'll see the result in Figure 8.7.

Figure 8.7

Sorting in reverse order.

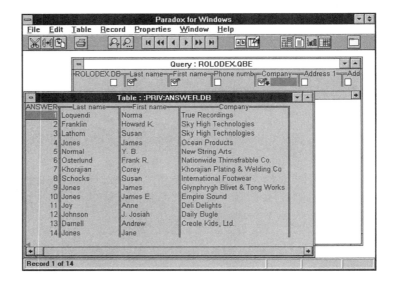

Note that if you use the Check Descending mark in a field other than the first and don't use the Sort Answer dialog box, the table will be sorted from left to right, as usual, *except for the field with the Check Descending mark*. In that field, only records that are the same as each other in all fields to the left of the descending field will be sorted in reverse order.

NOTE: Computer software is written by programmers instead of by normal people, so Z-to-A is considered descending order because the code number by which Z is represented to the computer is higher than the code number for A.

Saving the Results

There are two ways to save the results of a query. If you want to reuse the information in the ANSWER table *in its present form*, you can choose File Utilities Rename to rename the table, making it permanent. Bear in mind, however, that the renamed table has no intrinsic connection to the table from which the information was drawn. Changes made to the source table will not be reflected in the renamed table.

Saving an ANSWER Table

1. Choose File Utilities Rename.

Paradox displays the Table Rename dialog box.

2. Choose :PRIV:ANSWER.DB as the response for the Table field.

3. Enter the New name for the table.

4. Choose OK.

Paradox renames the table and all the members of its family, if there are any.

If you want a paper record of the result of a query, you can create a Quick Report.

Creating a Report from an ANSWER Table

1. Select the ANSWER table (by default, it will already be selected).

2. Press ⧈Shift + F7 , choose **T**able Quick Report, or click the Quick Report icon.

Paradox will produce a report on your printer, listing the items in the ANSWER table in columns headed by the field names.

Setting Search Conditions

Most commonly, when you want to get information from your database, you're interested in looking at the records that meet certain criteria you have in mind—not necessarily all the records in a particular field or set of fields. As the term *query by example* suggests, you tell Paradox what to look for by giving it an example. These examples can be a specific value, a range of values, something similar to a given value, or even several different values.

Before proceeding, add a field to the ROLODEX table, so that you have a bit more to work with:

1. Choose **F**ile Utilities Restructure.

2. Select the ROLODEX table and choose OK.

3. Move to the Notes field and press Ins .

4. Add a field called `Last contact`, and make it a Date-type field.

5. Choose Save.

When Paradox finishes restructuring the table, it displays the restructured table.

Imagine that this file is a list of clients that you contact monthly. Each time you complete a call to a client, you record the date in the new field. You might also make some notes in the Notes field. You will use a query to find out which clients are due for a call.

Press F9 or click the Edit icon to edit the table, and type dates (within the last two months) into the new field. The last part of your table should look something like Figure 8.8.

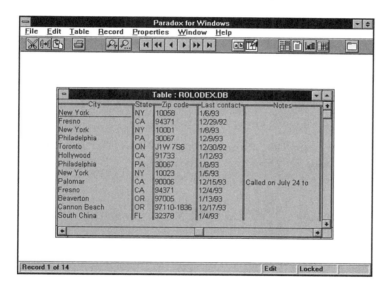

Figure 8.8
The Date field filled in.

Matching Specific Values

To match a specific value, move to the field (in the query table) in which it's located, and type the value you want Paradox to search for. Start with the Joneses again because there are so many of them. First clear the desktop with Window Close All. If asked whether you want to save it, choose No. Now choose File New Query, and choose the ROLODEX table again.

You already know that unless directed otherwise, Paradox shows only one instance of any given value. Thus, if you were to place a check mark in the Last name field and ask for *Jones*, you'd see just a single instance of the last name *Jones*. So place a check mark in both the Last name and First name fields.

Now you need to provide an example. Move to the Last name field and type `jones`. Execute the query. Surprise! You get an empty ANSWER table!

Why? Because unless you tell it otherwise, Paradox searches for an *exact* match of what you enter. All of your Joneses begin with an uppercase *J*. So go back to the query table and replace the lowercase *j* with an uppercase *J*. (You can either click the Field view icon or press F2 and move to the beginning of the field, or just click next to the *J*.)

While you're at it, go back to the First name field, and replace your check mark with a Check Plus (⇧Shift + F6). Remember, Paradox otherwise will show you only unique values, and you have more than one James Jones. Now when you press F8 or select Query Run, you should see an ANSWER table showing all of your Joneses, as Figure 8.9 illustrates.

> **NOTE:** If your ANSWER table is empty, either there are no values that match your query, or your query has an error in it. If there is an error, Paradox will display a message telling you so. Click the >> button for further details.

Finding Inexact Matches

To help you with situations of this type, Paradox has two quite different ways of finding *inexact* matches:

- The *like* operator.
- The wild-card characters you used with the **R**ecord Lo**c**ate **V**alue command.

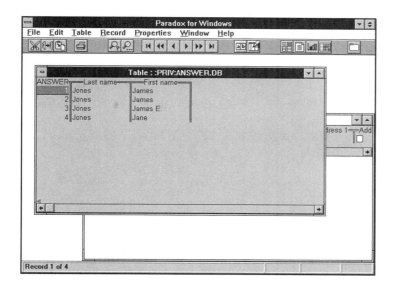

Figure 8.9
A properly constructed exact-match query.

Try the *like* operator first. Say you are writing a letter to Anne Joy and you can't remember how to spell her first name. You would type "like Ann" in the window in the First name column. After putting check marks in the check boxes of the fields you would like to see, press F8. Paradox will search for all values that resemble "Ann". The *like* operator always matches the first character of the value you give it to search for, and finds anything reasonably close. Your ANSWER table should now look like the one in Figure 8.10. It's a bit less precise than the exact match, but of course, that's what you requested. And it's quite useful when you're not exactly sure of the spelling of the item for which you're looking.

The wild-card characters @ and .. can also simplify searches when you're not sure what you're looking for. What was the name of that blivet and tong company? Something like Glenfree, wasn't it? But how do you spell it? Paradox can find it if you give it a reasonable approximation.

Go back to the query window and uncheck both checked fields. (You can do it by pressing F6 or by clicking in the boxes.) Delete any type that may be in the fields.

Figure 8.10
Finding an inexact match.

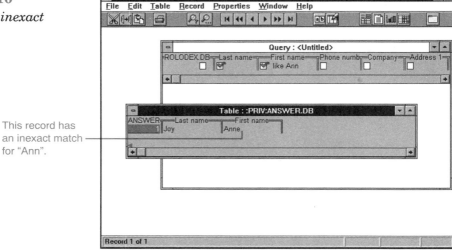

This record has
an inexact match
for "Ann".

Now place a check mark (F6) in the Company field check box, and type Gl@n.. Remember, the @ symbol replaces any character, and the double period (..) stands for any group of characters (or no characters). Run this query, and sure enough, your ANSWER table shows only the Company field, with the single entry Glynphrygh Blivet & Tong Works.

Finding Nonmatches

Suppose you want to find only records that *don't* match a certain value. To do so, use the *not* operator. The following steps will display everybody *except* the Joneses.

TIP: You can have more than one row in a query table. Use this fact to clear the previous query. Press ↓ to create a second "record." Then press ↑ to move back to the first "record" and delete it with Ctrl + Del , just as you would in a database table. This is faster than clearing all the specifications from a query table or closing the window and creating a new one.

Clear the previous query. The new query will resemble some of the earlier ones. Place a Check Plus mark in the First name field and a check mark in the Last name field. Now type `not Jones` into the Last name field and run the query. Your ANSWER table should show everything but the Joneses, as Figure 8.11 illustrates.

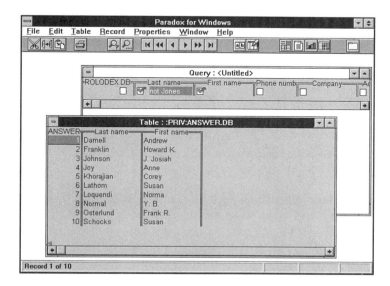

Figure 8.11
Using the not operator.

As another challenge to yourself, consider what would have happened if you had typed `not like jones` instead of `not Jones`.

Searching for Empty Fields

Why would you want to exclude certain values? You'll see why in the next example. Remember when you got a list of records sorted by Company? There was a blank record at the top of the list. If you wanted to see just that record, you could use the *blank* operator. Place a check mark in the Last name and First name fields, as shown in Figure 8.12. In the Company field, type the word `blank`.

Figure 8.12

Using the blank operator.

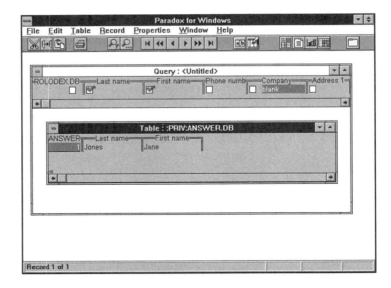

Notice that you *didn't* place a check mark in the Company field. This means that the Company field won't show up in the ANSWER table. (The field containing your selection criteria need not be displayed.) Since the Company field *should* be blank, why look at it?

When you run the query, your ANSWER table should look like the one in Figure 8.12. If you compare this result with Figure 8.6, you'll see that this is the record with no entry in the Company field.

Combining Operations

You're by no means restricted to a single operation per query. In the examples that follow in this chapter, you'll often use more than one criterion to select the information to display. The next exercise re-creates the ANSWER table shown in Figure 8.6, but without the blank records. You'll use both the *not* and *blank* operators.

In the query table, place a check mark in the Company field and change the text in that field to read `not blank`.

In other words, you've asked Paradox to include in the ANSWER table only those records whose Company field is not blank. You'll see, in Figure 8.13, the table you wanted to see in Figure 8.6.

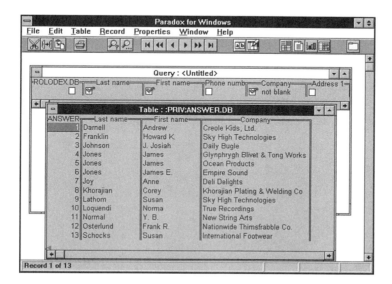

Figure 8.13
Excluding blank fields.

Changing Field Names

The names of the fields in the ANSWER table don't have to be the same as those in the query image. You might want to change them in order to use the changed names in reports based on your ANSWER table. To change field names, use the *as* operator. As an example, change the query now on the desktop so that the text in the Company field reads `not blank, as Firm`. When you run the revised query, the only change should be that the heading at the top of the first column now reads Firm instead of Company.

NOTE: A field will accept queries of up to 255 characters. If you can't see the entire query text, widen the field.

Notice also the comma in your new query. The comma separates several operations pertaining to a single field. If you leave out the comma, Paradox displays a warning dialog box with information about the nature of the error and its location. You must correct the error before Paradox can process the query.

Searching for Ranges of Values

Suppose you want not just a match, but everything over or under a certain value? For that, you use Paradox's *range operators*, which are listed below with their meanings.

=	Equal to (this is the default, and is optional)
>	Greater than
>=	Greater than or equal to
<	Less than
<=	Less than or equal to

You can use the range operators in any type of field. For example, you could search for only those companies whose names are in the first part of the alphabet by typing `<M.` into the Company field. The ANSWER table would then include only the record with no company name, plus

```
Creole Kids, Ltd.

Daily Bugle

Deli Delights

Empire Sound

Glynphrygh Blivet & Tong Works

International Footwear

Khorajian Plating & Welding Co
```

You could restrict the selection further by specifying both ends of the range. If you typed the search condition `<M, >G` into the Company field, your ANSWER table would include only the last three of the records in the previous table.

In the hypothetical example at the beginning of this chapter, you wanted a list of salespeople who had sold at least $25,000 worth of goods in any month. Assume that you have a table with each of your salespersons' sales figures for each month. You would put check marks in the Last name and First name fields, and type the formula `>=25000` into the Sales figures field. The resulting ANSWER table would display only the names of those of your sales staff who had met or exceeded the specified goal. If you wanted to see in which month they did so, you'd have to include that field as well. (NOTE: This isn't the best way to structure such a table.)

NOTE: When entering values in Numeric and Currency fields, you can enter only digits and decimal points. Commas and currency symbols are not allowed.

Try searching for a range of dates. Presumably, the dates you entered into your ROLODEX table aren't the same as those in mine, but let's use mine for the example. Suppose you wanted to find out which people you had last called in December. You'd set up the query as shown in Figure 8.14. I've rotated the fields so that you can see all the pertinent columns.

Note that both the beginning and the end of the range of dates have been specified, separated by commas. The search criteria could just as easily have been specified as `>11/30/92, <1/1/93`, but it would be a bit more confusing. The result, as you can see in the same figure, is an ANSWER table showing the names, phone numbers, and dates of last contact of those people you last called in December.

Using the Current Date

Paradox has a special operator for the current date: *today*. If you type `today` into a Date-type field, all records with today's date will appear in the ANSWER table. If a field of your order-processing database contains scheduled dates for various items, for example, you could use this feature to find the records to be processed on any given day.

Figure 8.14
Searching for a range of dates.

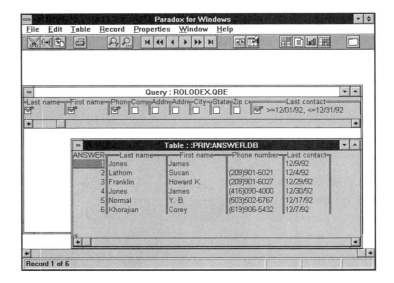

But the real value of the today operator lies in *date arithmetic*. Remember why you added the Date field to the ROLODEX table? It was to keep track of the last time you called each person listed. Your goal was to call each one monthly.

To find out who's actually due for a call, you need a list of the names and phone numbers of everyone you last called more than a month ago. To get those records, you need to find the ones with dates that are 30 days or more before today. The way to express this value in a Date field is `< today - 31`.

The actual number at the end of this expression will depend on the number of days in the previous month. In other words, you ask Paradox to display any date that is before (less than) 31 days before today's date. Figure 8.15 shows the query and the result when the query is processed on January 24,1993.

NOTE: You can leave out the spaces in expressions involving range operators. <today-31 would work equally well.

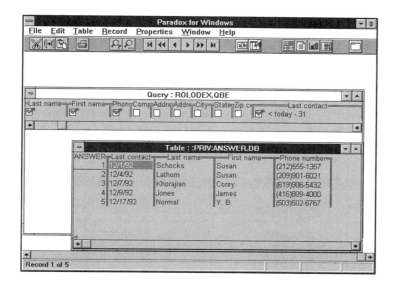

Figure 8.15
Date arithmetic using the today operator.

As you might surmise from the result, I've used the **Properties Answer Table Sort** command to sort the table by the date in the Last contact field. By rotating the ANSWER table and placing the Last contact field first, I've arranged my contacts in order by date, so I know which calls are most urgent.

Searching for More Than One Value

You can search for two or more different values in a field using the *or* operator. You know that most of your contacts are in New York and California. Suppose you want information on those two groups. Clear the query from the table, and place check marks (with F6) in the First name, Last name, Company, and State fields. Now, in the State field, type CA or NY.

CAUTION   When you've previously run a query that involved sorting the ANSWER table, be sure to choose Properties Answer Table Sort and choose OK before you set up a query that doesn't require the same sort order. This procedure will clear the Sort Answer dialog box.

The result, shown in Figure 8.16, includes the records of people in either of the selected states, but no others. When you use *or*, any value that matches either of the conditions you specify appears in the ANSWER table.

Figure 8.16
The or *operator.*

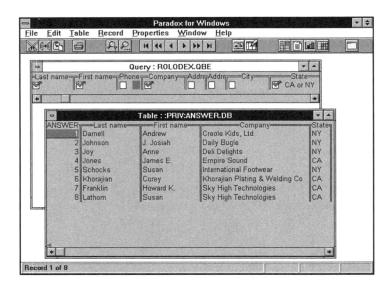

Similarly, you can use the comma to specify values in a single field that meet two different criteria. To see only the records for states *other* than New York and California, type `not CA, not NY` into the State field. You'll see the expected result in Figure 8.17.

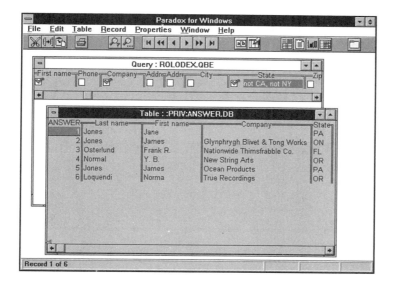

Figure 8.17

Combining two search conditions.

Another, quite different, technique allows you to search for several different values even if the values are not in the same field. To do so, set up several queries in the same query table, one for each item. Just make sure that you have check marks in all the columns to appear in the ANSWER table in *each* row of the query image.

Here's an example. Suppose you want to see these records:

- All the records of people named *Susan*.
- All the records from *Florida*.
- All the records of *Joneses* in *California*.

You'll need the Last name, First name, and State fields, so place check marks (F6) in those fields.

Now, you can't specify the search criteria as *Susan* in the First name column, *Jones* in the Last name column, and *FL* or *CA* in the State column, because that would pull up only records for people named *Susan Jones* from Florida or California. That's not what you're looking for. Instead, use three rows in the query table, as shown in Figure 8.18. Notice that each row specifies a different set of conditions.

Figure 8.18
Using multiple rows in a query statement.

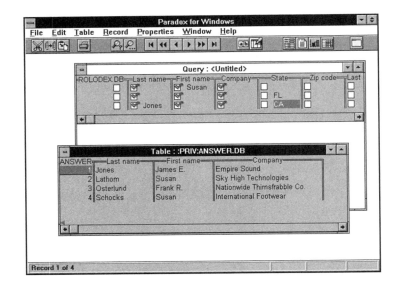

In the ANSWER table, also in Figure 8.18, the first condition (everyone whose first name is *Susan*) accounts for records 2 and 4; the second condition (everyone from *Florida*) accounts for record 3; and the third condition (*Joneses* from *California*) accounts for record 1.

Running a Query

1. Choose File New Query.

Paradox displays the Select File dialog box.

2. Select a table name from the list and choose OK.

Paradox displays a query window, which contains a table with the same fields as the one you selected, except that it's empty. The window title reveals its character.

3. Place check marks, Check Plus marks, or check descending marks in the check boxes in the fields you want to see in your ANSWER table.

If you use check marks, Paradox displays all unique values in the field. If you use Check Plus marks, Paradox displays all matching values in the field. If you use check-descending marks, Paradox displays the matching values in reverse order.

4. Enter the values for which you wish to search into the appropriate fields.

5. Press F8, or choose Query Run, or click the Run Query icon.

Paradox either displays the values you requested in an ANSWER table or displays a dialog box indicating an error in the way the query image is set up.

NOTE: You may use any of the query operators, or wild-card characters, to specify the type of match you want.

NOTE: If an error message appears, go back to the referenced field and correct the query. Re-run the query.

For reference, the basic operators used in queries are summarized in Table 8.1. Those operators used only in queries that calculate new values will be found in Table 9.1, in Chapter 9.

Table 8.1

Query Operators

Operator	Effect
like	Finds all values similar to the search criterion.
not	Finds all values that do not match the search criterion.
blank	Finds all records with no value entered in the field.
today	Finds all records with today's date entered in the field; allows date arithmetic based on today's date.
or	Finds all values that match either of the conditions specified.
,	Finds all values that match both of the conditions specified.
as	Changes the name of the field in the ANSWER table.
>	Specifies all values greater than the given value.
>=	Specifies all values greater than or equal to the given value.
<	Specifies all values less than the given value.
<=	Specifies all values less than or equal to the given value.
=	Specifies all values that are the same as the given value (the default).
..	When placed before or after a group of characters, finds a value with any characters preceding or following the specified characters.
@	Finds a value with any character in the position of the @ symbol.

Save a Query

1. Choose File Save or File Save As.
2. Type the name for the query file in the **N**ew File Name text box, and choose OK.

Add Existing Records to a Table with an Unlike Structure

1. Create a query window for the source table.
2. Choose Query Add Table or click the Add Table icon.
3. Select the target table and choose OK.
4. Select the far left column of the target table and press ⏎.
5. Place example elements in each field of the source table that you want to appear in the target table.
6. Place the example elements in the fields of the target table where you want the elements of the source table to appear.
7. Run the query.

Queries to Create New Values and Change Data

In this chapter, you'll learn how to use existing values to derive new values that don't appear in your database. The techniques you learn here will not change any of the values in your source database, only in your ANSWER table.

You'll also learn some query techniques to change the values in your database. You can use queries to add, change, and delete records—three of the most fundamental processes of database management.

Calculating New Values

Paradox gives you many ways to create ANSWER tables that have new values not found in the source table. One of the most powerful is the *calc* operator. This operator tells Paradox to perform some type of calculation. It has two uses:

- To perform arithmetic operations on Number, Date, or Currency fields.

- To combine the values found in Alphanumeric fields.

You'll learn both uses of this operator.

The basic technique is to create an expression containing either the value to be changed or a symbol representing the value to be changed (an example element) and one of the operators found in Table 9.1. The result will be placed in a separate column of the ANSWER table. (The nonarithmetic query operators at the end of Table 9.1 are used for performing calculations that are beyond the scope of this book and are included for reference only.)

Table 9.1
Query Calculation Operators

Operator	Function
+	Adds numeric values or concatenates alphanumeric values on each side of the operator.
–	Subtracts the value following the sign.
*	Multiplies values.
/	Divides by the value following the / sign.
( )	Groups values for arithmetic operations.
sum	Finds the sum of the values in a field.
average	Finds the average of the values in a field.
count	Displays the number of values in the field.
min	Finds the lowest value in a field.
max	Finds the highest value in a field.
all	Modifies the sum or average operator to include all values in the field, whether or not they are unique.
unique	Modifies the sum or average operator to include only one instance of any non-unique values.

Entering Example Elements

In order to use the *calc* operator on more than one field, you must use an *example element*. An example element is an *arbitrary value* that stands for any value in the field. For example, you might use Q to stand for any first name, and X to stand for any last name. You can then use any of the arithmetic operators listed in Table 9.1 to perform an arithmetic operation on the values represented by the example elements.

To enter an example element, you select the field where it is to appear and press F5, the Example key. An editing cursor appears. This is your cue to type a dummy value. The value will appear in red to distinguish it from the search conditions you've been entering up to now.

Example elements have two purposes:

- To tell Paradox to do something to any value in the field in which it appears.

- To link fields in one table to those in another in a query involving two or more tables.

Now you'll learn to use example elements in calculations.

Without example elements in a calculated expression, you're simply doing arithmetic. If you use an expression such as

```
calc 25000 + 100
```

all records in the ANSWER table have the value 25100 in the field where the expression appears. If you replace the value 25000 with a dummy value, on the other hand, Paradox adds 100 to every value in the field.

TIP: If you make a mistake entering an example element, you can delete it with Ctrl + ◆Backspace. Once you delete an example element, however, you have to press F5 again to enter a new one.

Example elements with calculations are invaluable in an application such as preparing invoices. You can use two example elements, one for the number of items ordered and another for the unit price, to calculate the total cost. You then can use an expression such as

```
calc (total * 1.06)
```

to calculate the price with sales tax of 6% added. In this section, you'll see how to place such information into new fields which don't exist in your source table.

A single field in a query table can contain up to 255 characters. This means that calculation expressions can be up to 255 characters unless there are other items, such as selection criteria or example elements, in the field. Calculations follow the standard order of precedence. Items in parentheses are calculated first. After that, multiplication and division are performed before addition and subtraction. If all calculations in an expression are of equal precedence, calculations are performed from left to right.

Performing Arithmetic Operations

Now you'll learn to set up a calculated value with an example element. First choose Window Close All to clear the desktop. Next choose File New Query and select the Rolodex table. Now follow these Quick Steps.

Setting Up a Calculation

1. You may find it helpful to rotate the fields so that you can see all the ones you'll want to use. (In this instance, move to the Company field and press Ctrl+R six times.)

2. Use F6 or click the check box to place check marks in the fields you want to include in your query (in this instance First name, Last name, and Phone number).

3. Move to the appropriate fields and press F5 to enter any example elements you'll need (in this instance, move to the Last contact field).

4. Type `a` to use the letter *a* as an example element.

5. To enter a calculation, type `, calc` to separate the example element from an expression and tell Paradox to calculate a new value.

6. Press F5 to enter an example element on which to perform the calculation.

7. Re-enter the element you just entered (`a`).

8. Type the calculation to be performed (in this instance, `+30 as Next Call`).

The entry fields should appear as shown in Figure 9.1.

In this strange formula, you've told Paradox to take all the values in the Last contact field, add 30 to them, and place them into a new field called *Next Call*. If you didn't give the field a new name, it would be called, quite logically, `Last contact +30`.

Figure 9.1
Setting up a calculation.

An example calculation

Run the query. As you can see in Figure 9.2, the ANSWER table now includes a field called *Next Call*. All the records from the ROLODEX table are present, with new dates in the new field. The new dates are a month later than the dates in the ROLODEX table. You can press ⇧Shift+F7 (Instant Report) to print a report of the ANSWER table, and then copy the new dates into your calendar.

Figure 9.2
The result of a calculation.

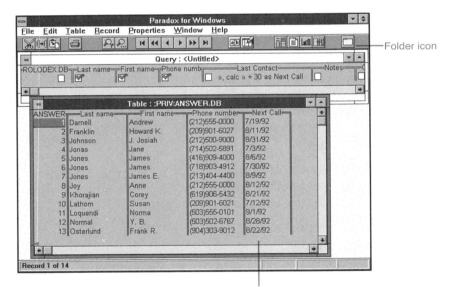

Folder icon

New field added with the calculation results

Note that *you have not changed the original ROLODEX table in any way*. You can, in fact, change the data in a table using queries, as you'll learn later in this chapter.

Saving Queries

You might want to create the ANSWER table with the Next call field every week. But it's a bit of a nuisance to set up, and you might forget a step or make a mistake the next time you tried to create it. Fortunately, once you have a query that works, you can save it.

Now that you have a working query, use the following Quick Steps to save it.

Saving a Query

1. Choose **File Save** or **File Save As**.

   Paradox displays the Save File As dialog box.

2. Type the name for the query file in the **N**ew File Name text box.

3. Choose OK.

   Paradox saves your query in a file with the name you entered and the extension .QBE.

Follow these steps and enter `calls` as the name for the new query table. Now you can repeat this query at any time by choosing **File O**pen **Q**uery, selecting the file, and choosing OK.

This command will bring the query form you just used to the desktop. Run the query to complete the calculation.

TIP: If there are no windows open on the desktop, you can select a query by clicking the Open Query icon.

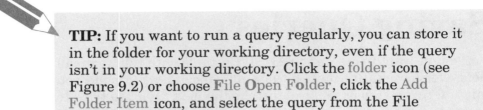

TIP: If you want to run a query regularly, you can store it in the folder for your working directory, even if the query isn't in your working directory. Click the folder icon (see Figure 9.2) or choose File Open Folder, click the Add Folder Item icon, and select the query from the File Browser.

Calculations on Several Fields

You can use example elements to refer to the values in more than one field in a calculation expression. In doing so, you can derive new values based on the values in several fields—sums, averages, and so on.

You can also combine the text found in several Alphanumeric fields into a new field that Paradox will create for that purpose. Let's look at arithmetic operations first.

Arithmetic Operations Combining Several Fields

Suppose you had a table of sales records structured like the one shown in Figure 9.3, listing the sales figures for six consecutive months. (This is far from the ideal way to structure such a table, but it will do for an example.)

You would have sales figures for each salesperson for each month in the appropriate field. You'd like to find out the average monthly sales of each member of your sales staff. To do so, you would:

1. Create a query based on this table.

2. Place check marks in the name fields.

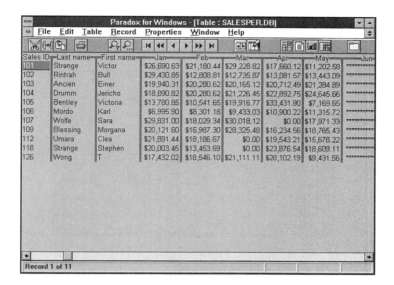

Figure 9.3

A table of sales records.

3. Press F5 and enter a, b, c, d, e, and f, respectively, into each of the six monthly fields as example elements.

4. Enter the formula shown in Figure 9.4 in one of the empty fields.

5. Run the query.

You now get a table like the one in Figure 9.4, showing each salesperson's average. This formula simply adds the values represented by the six example elements and divides the sum by 6. The parentheses ensure that the division is performed on the sum, not simply on the last value.

TIP: If you're moving from one field to the next with the keyboard, press F5 twice to activate the cursor and enter an example element.

Figure 9.4

Calculating the average of several fields.

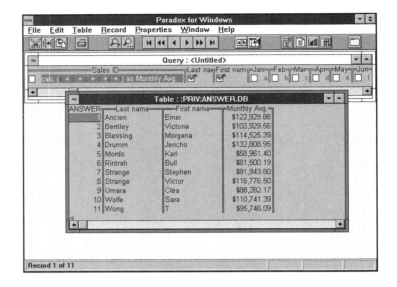

Concatenating Alphanumeric Fields

Suppose you want to print a series of mailing labels or create a file to use for a mass mailing. The data in the ROLODEX table can be used to create five-line name and address labels.

Now, if you just use the fields as they appear, you'll get a lot of blank spaces between the first and last name and between the city and state, because Paradox will allocate enough space to hold an entire field. To get rid of the extra spaces, you can combine, or *concatenate*, the fields to produce a new value.

The following exercise creates two concatenated values—one combining the data in the First name and Last name fields, and the second combining the City, State, and Zip code fields, with a comma inserted at the appropriate point. As you'll see, when you concatenate alphanumeric data, you can also add characters that are not part of any field. Indeed, you may want to use this technique just to add characters to an existing field.

Clear the desktop, and create a new ROLODEX query table. (By now, the old one is so out of kilter that you need a fresh start.)

You'll need five example elements. Remember, to distinguish an example element from a search criterion, you press F5 before entering the example element. Enter the following example elements in the specified fields:

Last name	a
First name	b
City	c
State	s
Zip code	z

Remember, the actual content of the example element can be completely arbitrary. I've used *c*, *s*, and *z* simply for mnemonic purposes. Click the check boxes in the Company, Address 1, and Address 2 fields. Now you're ready for the hard part.

When a calculation produces a new field, you can place the calculation in any field in the query table. In the Company field, type the formula

```
calc b +" "+ a as Name
```

Remember that b and a are example elements. To enter them, you press F5 first. Press Spacebar after each, and the red highlight disappears, allowing you to enter the formula. The last part of the formula gives the new field a new name.

The formula tells Paradox to create a new field called Name, containing the value from the First name field (represented by *b*), followed by a space, followed by the value from the Last name field (represented by *a*).

Now, in the Address 1 field, you're going to create a single field for the City, State, and Zip code. Enter the formula

```
calc c + ", " + s + " " + z as Address 3
```

Notice that the comma which separates City and State appears *within* the quotation marks. Otherwise it would be interpreted as a separator between two search conditions.

Remember, once again, that the c, s, and z are example elements, entered by pressing F5. Figure 9.5 shows the formulas you've entered.

Figure 9.5

Concatenating Alphanumeric fields.

> **TIP:** Use quotation marks to surround a value entered in a search condition whenever the value you're searching for contains a character or command that would otherwise be interpreted as a command by Paradox. To search for someone with the last name of *Blank*, for example, you can type `"Blank"` into the Last name field, so Paradox won't search for empty records. Similarly, to search the ROLODEX table for *Creole Kids, Ltd.*, you'd have to enclose the search criterion in quotation marks in order to include the comma.

When you run the query, Paradox combines the values as you requested, placing them into the fields you named, as shown in Figure 9.6. You'll have to rotate the fields to get them into the right order for printing labels, but you already know how to do that. Again, the values in your original table are not affected by this procedure.

Using the Editing Operators

You now know how to use queries to find information in your databases, and how to calculate new values based on those contained in the databases. Now you'll learn to use queries to add, change, and delete records. This is done with special commands called *editing operators*. The techniques you'll learn next use a different method of constructing queries: placing commands in the far left column. As you become more familiar with Paradox, you'll find that many advanced queries use a similar technique—those involving *groups* or *sets* of records, for example. However, operations of this type are beyond the scope of this book.

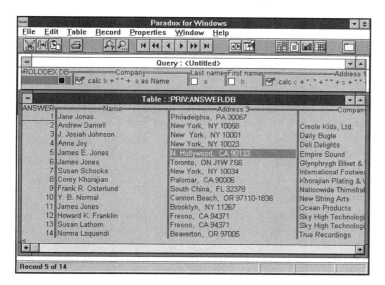

Figure 9.6

The result of concatenating alphanumeric fields.

Finding Specific Values

The simplest of these operations is finding a specific record. You've already seen how to find a value in a field with the Zoom key (Ctrl + Z) or with the **R**ecord Lo**c**ate **V**alue command. The **F**ind operator is a somewhat more sophisticated version of the same thing. Open a query window and press F . The word Find will appear in the far left column of the table, beneath the table name. Then type the values to find in any fields you wish to specify.

TIP: Using a find query is the easiest way to find a record you want to edit in a large table.

The advantage of this method over using the Zoom key or the **R**ecord Lo**c**ate **V**alue command is that you can specify a value in more than one field at a time. For example, you know that you have more than one Susan and more than one entry for Sky High Technologies. To find the record containing both values, follow the Quick Steps below to set up and run the query shown in Figure 9.7.

Finding a Record Based on Values in Several Fields

1. In the leftmost column, press F.

Paradox enters the word Find.

2. Move to the first field containing a value to search for, and enter it (wild cards are permitted). In this example, enter Susan in the First name field.

3. Move to the next field containing a value to search for, and enter it. In this example, enter Sky.. in the Company field.

4. Repeat step 3 as many times as necessary to specify the record you're seeking.

5. Press F8 to run the query.

Paradox displays an ANSWER table containing only the requested record.

You can now press F9 (Edit) to make any needed changes and update the source table with the **F**ile **T**able Utilities **A**dd command.

Figure 9.7
A find query.

Paradox lets you know you're using
the Find operator.

Deleting Records with a Query

Now that you've tried one editing operator, try something just a little more dangerous. Don't worry, there's a way to back out. You can delete records matching any criteria you specify by placing the **D**elete operator in the far left column and then entering the criteria. You specify the search criteria exactly the same way you did to **F**ind information.

This technique is especially useful for deleting records with dates earlier than a certain date. For example, you may want to drop customers from your mailing list who haven't placed an order in two years.

To delete their records, you would create a query table for the appropriate database, and press D. The word **D**elete appears in the far left column. Type the value <= today - 730 in the Last order column. (The number 730 represents two 365-day years.)

To see the effects of the **D**elete operator on the ROLODEX table, delete all the records of people from New York from the table. Follow these steps:

1. Create a new row in the query table by pressing ↓.

2. Press ↑ and delete the old query by pressing Ctrl+Del.

3. Move to the leftmost column and press D.

4. Type NY in the State column.

5. Run the query.

As you can see in Figure 9.8, the deleted records are not spirited off into limbo, but are stored in a new temporary table called DELETED. As you can see on the status bar, the ROLODEX table now has only nine records, instead of 14. The records in the DELETED table are truly gone from the source table.

Figure 9.8
A delete query.

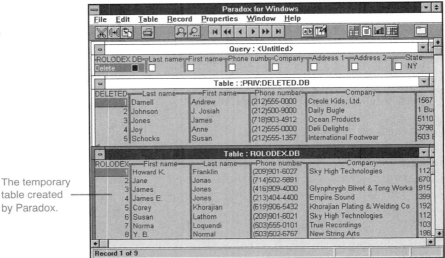

The temporary table created by Paradox.

To save a table of deleted records choose File Table Utilities Rename to give the table a new name. You might want to do that with your hypothetical old customers so that you can get them back again if they placed a new order. Or more significantly, when processing a day's orders or shipments, this is the first step toward storing the day's records in a history file.

Undoing a Delete Query

For now, you want to get the deleted records back. Remember, you can add records from one table to another if their structures are the same. Since the DELETED table is taken directly from the ROLODEX table, it has the same structure. Therefore, you can restore the records to the ROLODEX table using the File Table Utilities Add command.

The source table is :PRIV:DELETED.DB, and the target table is ROLODEX.DB. Choose Append as the method to use.

> When you're replacing deleted records, you don't   CAUTION
> want to make changes to the existing records. If
> you use **U**pdate, you might actually replace some records
> in the target table. However, with Append, the worst that
> can happen is that you'll have some key violations in a
> KEYVIOL table.

If you choose View Target Table in the Options section, you'll see that you now have all 14 records again, and they are in their original order. As with most temporary tables, however, the DELETED table is not emptied by this procedure. If you want to do some further work with the deleted records, you can.

> **NOTE:** As a rule, it's safer to edit your records in place
> than to delete them and reinsert them. However, if the
> power goes off, your DELETED table won't be gone. It will
> be saved in your private directory (as are all temporary
> query results) with a name of the form _QBE*n*.DB, where
> *n* is a number. The query tables themselves are saved in
> files with names of the form __Q*nnnnn*.DB. In any case, no
> window that's on your desktop will be deleted until you
> close it.

Adding Records with a Query

You've just reviewed how to add records from one table to another when their structures are the same. Paradox also allows you to add records from one table to another when their structures differ.

The restriction, obviously, is that the table to which records are to be added must have appropriate fields for at least some of the data in the source table.

The basic procedure is to set up *two* query tables, one for the source table and another for the target, and to place the *same* example element in equivalent fields in each of the tables. This correspondence tells Paradox into which fields to insert the data from the source table. Finally, move to the leftmost column of the *target* table and press ⎣I⎦ to enter the word **I**nsert. This is our first example of a multi-table query.

You have a perfect opportunity already on disk: You can add the people from the ROLODEX table to the Customer database. Since you borrowed the structure of the ROLODEX table when you created the CUSTOMER table, you know they have at least some fields with similar structures.

As you may recall, all the fields in the ROLODEX table are Alphanumeric except Last contact, which is a Date, and Notes, which is a Memo. All the fields in the CUSTOMER table are also Alphanumeric, except for Initial order (a Date field) and Credit limit (a Currency field).

The CUSTOMER table has a few more fields than the ROLODEX table, but there is an equivalent field in the CUS-TOMER table for every field in the ROLODEX table except the Notes field. (Last contact and Initial order aren't equivalent logically, but since they are both Date-type fields, you can treat them as equivalent.)

Filling Out the Query Forms

To complete this procedure, you need to create a relationship between the fields in your source table and the fields in the target table into which the data should be placed. To do so, use example elements. Remember, example elements merely indicate the data in a field generically, they do not stand for any particular values. Also, they can be completely arbitrary, although they need not be.

Start by opening a new query window, with the ROLODEX table in it. Next, use the Query Add Table command or click the Add Table icon (see Figure 9.9) to open a query table for the CUSTOMER table. It will appear below the ROLODEX query table, in the same window. (Now you know why query windows contain all that white space.)

Enter example elements as indicated in Table 9.2, which indicates the relationship between the fields in the two tables. (Press F5 before typing each example element.) Note that some fields have no example elements. These are the fields that the two tables don't have in common.

Table 9.2

Example Elements and Equivalences for the ROLODEX and CUSTOMER Tables

Rolodex Field	Example Element	Customer Field Cust. ID
Last name	a	Last name
First name	b	First name
Phone number	p	Phone number
		Department
Company	c	Company
Address 1	d	Street address
Address 2	e	Suite no. or P.O. box
City	f	City
State	s	State
Zip code	z	Zip or Postal code
		Country
Last contact	date	Initial order
Notes		
		Credit limit

Select the far left column of the CUSTOMER query table and press ⎵. This will place the **I**nsert command in that column.

I can't show you the complete query tables, but the far left screen columns appear in Figure 9.9. (I've reduced the column widths so you can see more of them.) Remember, if your example elements are not in red, they *aren't* example elements. Paradox will treat them as search criteria and get very confused.

Figure 9.9
*Setting up an
insert query.*

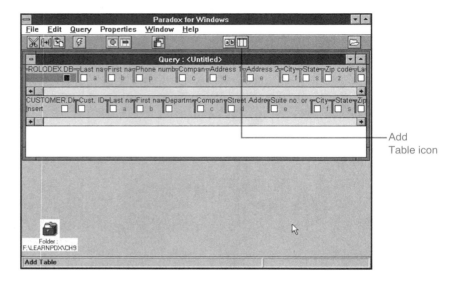

Add
Table icon

When a given example element appears in fields in different tables, it creates a link between those tables, telling Paradox to treat the fields with the same example element as equivalent fields.

All set? Run the query. When Paradox finishes processing the query, you'll see two new tables—one called INSERTED, containing only one record, and a second called ERRORINS, with the remaining records. These tables appear in Figure 9.10.

Naturally, the INSERTED table contains a copy of the records that were actually inserted (as you can verify by viewing the CUSTOMER table). The other table contains errors from the insert query.

Why weren't the other 13 records inserted? Remember that the Cust. ID field is a key field. That means every record must have a unique value in that field.

Since the ROLODEX table doesn't have an equivalent field, all the records to be inserted have a blank in that field. The

CUSTOMER table can have only one such record. Thus it rejects all but one of the records. In this instance, the ERRORINS table is more or less equivalent to a KEYVIOL table. In the following section, you'll treat the ERRORINS table as you would treat a KEYVIOL table.

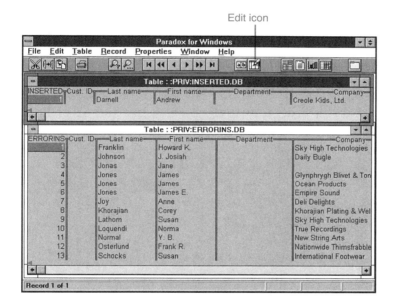

Edit icon

Figure 9.10
The results of an insert query.

Completing the Procedure

You'll need the additional customer records for examples in later chapters, so you have to get the records from the ERRORINS table into the CUSTOMER table. The only factor that prevents your adding the records is that they don't have proper keys.

To solve this problem, select the ERRORINS table, and press F9 to edit it. Move to the Cust. ID field, and type 00003, pressing ↓ when you finish. You'll move down to the second record in the table. Type 00004. Continue down the column, increasing the number by 1, until you reach record 13. The value in that record should be 00015. Press F9 or click the Edit icon when you're finished.

Now use the File Table Utilities Add command to add the records from :PRIV:ERRORINS.DB to CUSTOMER.DB. This time it doesn't matter which option you choose—Append, Update, or Append & Update. Be sure to place a check mark in the View Target Table check box.

The final step is to edit the CUSTOMER table, which is now the selected table on the desktop. Press F9 or click the Edit icon (see Figure 9.10) to edit the table and type 00016 in the first record, the one with the blank Cust. ID field. Press F9 or click the Edit icon when you're done. The result appears in Figure 9.11. You'll note that the record you just edited will move to the end of the table, because Paradox sorts the records in order according to the values in the key fields.

Figure 9.11

*Adding the
updated records.*

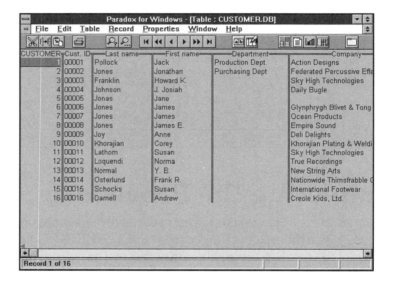

Altering Values with a Query

Now you'll learn how to use a query to make global changes to the values in a field. To do this, you use the *CHANGETO* operator.

Unlike the other editing operators, Changeto is not placed in the far left column. In fact, Changeto queries resemble normal search queries. However, in common with the other editing operators, Changeto requires no checked fields. You'll perform several Changeto operations before you're through so that you can taste the power of the Changeto operator. The basic principle is simple. You simply enter a formula in the form of

```
oldvalue, changeto newvalue
```

in the field containing the old value. Your newly expanded CUSTOMER table now has 16 records. (Granted, the Last call dates have been miraculously transformed into the dates of the new customers' first orders.) But the customers all need Credit limits as well.

Making Global Changes

Let's assume that $2,000.00 is the company's minimum credit limit, and assign it to all the new customers. Keep the CUSTOMER table on the desktop so you can watch the changes as they occur.

Next, create a new query window for the CUSTOMER table. In the Credit limit field, type `blank, changeto 2000`. This tells Paradox to place the value 2,000 into any record in which this field is blank. When the entry is correct, run the query.

A new, temporary table called CHANGED will appear with all the records that were originally in the Rolodex file. At the same time, the value $2,000.00 will appear in all the blank fields in the CUSTOMER table. In Figure 9.12, I've displayed the CUSTOMER and CHANGED tables, along with the query. I've also resized the windows and rotated the fields, so you can compare the two tables. As you can see, in the CHANGED table, the Credit limit field is still blank.

NOTE: When Paradox changes a value in a record, it saves the old version of the record in the CHANGED table. As with inserted and deleted records, this gives you a chance to edit the results or to undo the change if you made a mistake.

Figure 9.12
Globally changing an empty field.

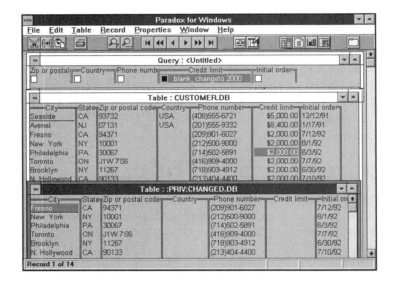

Changing Values Based on Values in Another Field

The Changeto operator can perform even more complex tasks. For example, you know you have one record from Canada. But the Country field is blank for all the records you inserted. The form of a Canadian postal code is different than a Zip code. You can use that information to give the Canadian record its proper Country designation.

Add a new line to the query table and delete the current line. Now move to the Zip or Postal code field. Type this text:

@@@ @@@

This is a wild-card pattern of any three characters, followed by a space, followed by any three characters. A postal code will match that pattern, but not a Zip code. Now, in the Country field, type `changeto Canada`. You see the results in Figure 9.13.

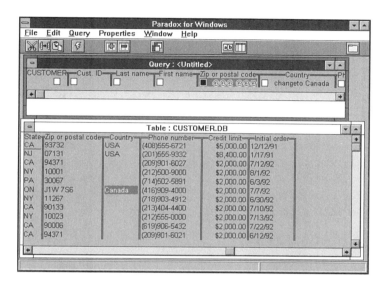

Figure 9.13
Changing values in a different field.

Processing Several Changes at Once

You can process several changes at once by using separate lines in your query table. Assume, for example, that customers who have been with the company for three months deserve a credit increase of 40 percent, and those who have been customers for two months deserve an increase of 20 percent. Select the customers by the values in their Initial order field. You'll have to set ranges of dates to look for, and use example elements to change the Credit limit.

Close the query window and open a new one for the CUSTOMER table. In the Initial order field, type

```
< today - 30, > today - 60
```

This sets the range of dates for which you'll grant a 20 percent increase as more than 30 but less than 60 days before today's date. Now press ⤶ to create another line. On this line in the same field, type

```
<= today - 60, > today - 90
```

This formula selects the group for the 40 percent increase as at least 60 but less than 90 days before today's date.

Now move to the first line of the Credit limit field. Press F5 to enter an example element. It can be anything. (I used *limit*.) Follow the example element with a comma and the *Changeto* operator, so your entry looks like limit, changeto. Type the example element again followed by * 1.20 to multiply the current value by 1.20. On the second line, use a *different* example element (*curr*) and repeat the procedure, changing the last part of the command to * 1.40 so your entry looks like

```
curr, changeto curr * 1.40
```

(If you use the same example element on both lines, the query will affect the same values twice.) You can see both the proper form for the query and the result (assuming the date is September 12, 1992) in Figure 9.14.

Figure 9.14

Multiple changes with example elements.

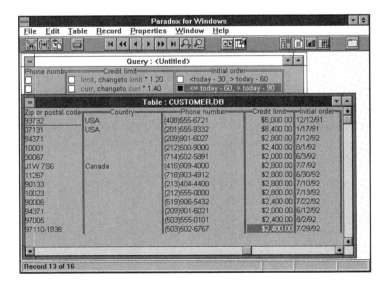

In the exercises you've just completed, you've barely begun to tap the power of the Paradox editing operators. As your mastery of these operators increases, you will find many more ways to use them.

Defining Referential Integrity

1. Select File Table Utilities Restructure or Table Restructure.
2. Select Referential Integrity from the Table Properties list box.
3. Select Define.
4. From the Table column, choose the parent table to which you want to link the current table.
5. From the Fields column, choose the field(s) that match the key.

Linking a Lookup Table

1. Select File Table Utilities Restructure or Table Restructure.
2. Select Table Lookup from the Table Properties list box.
3. Select Define.
4. From the Lookup Table column, choose the parent table containing the source data.
5. From the Fields column, select the common field.

Rules for Multi-Table Applications

- Don't store an item of information in more than one place unless it's a linking field.
- Link tables using key fields.
- If you must link more than one detail record to a single record in a master table, use multiple-field keys in the detail table.
- Keep the number of fields in a stable small. Use linked tables to store repeating information.
- KISS (Keep it simple, stupid!).

Chapter
10

Creating Relationships Between Tables

Up to now, you've been working with records in a single file. However, as you may remember from Chapter 1, Paradox is a relational database. The true power of Paradox lies in how well it handles data organized into a group of related files.

You've already gotten a small taste of working with several tables in completing an Insert query. In this chapter, I'll present a multi-table order entry application using the CUSTOMER table as a starting point. In ensuing chapters, you'll see how Paradox's power makes this application work.

Setting up a multi-table application takes both planning and experimentation. Don't be surprised if it doesn't immediately work the way you want. However, the procedures, at least in the first stages, are the same as those for setting up a single-table application. Only the logic is different.

You have to approach your data from a different point of view. Ideally, you want as little redundancy as possible.

Therefore, the most important design principle is a simple one: *Don't store an item of information in more than one place.* There's one very important exception to this principle, as you'll see later in this chapter.

In the following pages, I'll describe the application first, so that you can see what's to be accomplished. After that, I'll explain how to set it up. Then I'll explain the theory behind the setup, and how Paradox handles an application of this type.

Why Use Multiple Tables?

The application we'll look at is an automated, on-line, order-entry system for a hypothetical mail-order office and computer supply company called SuperService Supply Co. It updates your inventory files and your billing files. It also allows your order clerks to check the inventory while ordering to ensure that items are in stock and that the item numbers are accurate.

What Information Do You Need?

Think about the items of information that should appear on the order form. Obviously, you'll want to have your company name and address, but that will be the same for all orders so you needn't worry about it. You'll want the customer's complete name and address for billing and shipping purposes. The header of your order should include:

- The order number.
- The date.
- Some way of identifying the salesperson.
- The method of shipping requested by the customer.

You'll need a series of detail lines, each of which shows:

- The catalog number of the item ordered.
- A description of the item ordered.
- The quantity of the item ordered.
- The unit price of the item.
- The extension, or unit price multiplied by the quantity.

In addition, you'll want some summary fields which would be calculated at the time of the order, for example:

- Total cost of the items ordered.
- Shipping charge.
- Sales tax, if any.
- Grand total.

Assume that the shipping charge is included automatically, so you don't have to think about it. The resulting order form might look like Figure 10.1.

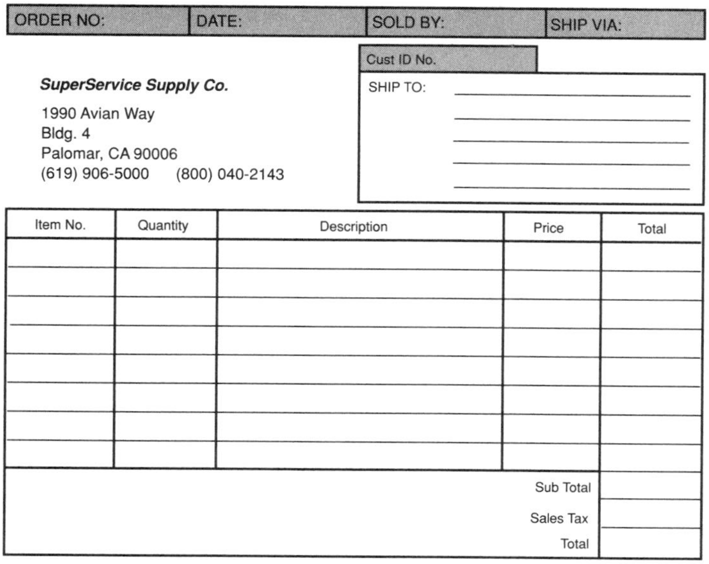

Figure 10.1

An order form.

What Database Fields Do You Need?

Now this information must be translated into database fields. The primary table will be called ORDERS. If the application were contained in a single file, you might want all the information from your CUSTOMER table (except the Initial order and Credit limit fields) plus all of the following. (I've grouped the fields conceptually, to make it easier to see the relationships among them.)

Order Information

> Order Number
>
> Sold by
>
> Date
>
> Ship via

Detail Items

> Item number
>
> Quantity sold
>
> Description
>
> Unit price
>
> Extension

Summary Items

> Subtotal
>
> Sales tax
>
> Total

Limiting Redundancy

Now, if your table had all these fields, you'd have to include the complete customer information in each record, along with the detail items for every item ordered. There are several things wrong with that picture:

- It violates the first principle: Data for each customer appears many times in the same table.

- The resulting file will be very large.

- You won't be able to calculate the summary items, because each record will include the information on only one item purchased.

The solution is to create a series of linked tables. One, which you already have, contains the customer information. Another contains the items unique to each order: the combination of order number, date, salesperson, and shipping method. A third holds all the detail items. When you complete an order, you'll pull in the information about your customers from the CUSTOMER table and information about the detail lines from your inventory database.

Now where do you put the summary information? It might go into the order file. However, Paradox can calculate these items for you whenever you need them. Moreover, your data is more likely to be current if you calculate these items as needed.

Structuring the Data

So how do you get the information from the CUSTOMER table into the order? And how do you look up items in the inventory? More to the point, how will anyone know which detail lines belong to which order? The solution is to create a *data model* which explains (both to you and to Paradox) the relationship between the items. The data model is shown schematically in Figure 10.2. (You'll actually create this data model in Chapter 11. In this chapter, you'll complete some preliminary steps.)

In the figure, the links are indicated by lines connecting a field in one table to a field in another. You'll notice that each table has one field in common with a table to which it's linked. (Shaded fields are key fields.)

Figure 10.2
*Four linked tables
for an order-entry
application.*

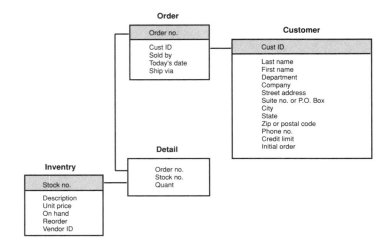

Linking the Tables

Think for a moment about the logic of this arrangement. The ORDERS table is your master table. It contains a duplicate of the Cust. ID field from the CUSTOMER table. Remember, you set up the CUSTOMER table so that this field was unique (which it must be if it's a key field) and arbitrary.

Customer Information

Thus, the unique Cust. ID number can appear in only one customer's record in the CUSTOMER table. Given access to this single item, Paradox can pull in all the information you need about a given customer, because Paradox will know which record to get.

Getting Inventory Data

Similarly, the DETAIL table is linked to the INVENTRY table by means of the Stock no. field. Again, this is a unique and arbitrary item. As you can see, it's a key field in the INVENTRY table. Once you have the stock number, you can quickly find out the correct description, the price, and the number of items on hand, because Paradox uses that item to find the correct record.

Linking the Details to the Master Table

Finally, records in the DETAIL table are linked to the order to which they refer by the Order no. field. Notice that this is a key field in the master table, but not in the DETAIL table.

A record in the DETAIL table contains only three items. In fact, the only unique item in the DETAIL table is the quantity ordered. Thus, the DETAIL table serves as a link between the ORDERS table and the INVENTRY table.

One-to-Many Relationships

But won't you run into a problem because you've stored the Order no., Stock no., and Cust. ID in two places each? No, because you've repeated only enough information to find all the items you need. These are the fields that link the tables.

If you've planned your application correctly, you may have many records in the subordinate tables linked to a single record in the master table. (This, in database parlance, is a *one-to-many* relationship.)

In order to establish such a relationship in Paradox, the linking fields in the subordinate tables *must* be key fields. Since you are using the Order no. field to link the detail records to the master table, it must be a key field in the DETAIL table.

But if Order no. were the *only* key field in the DETAIL table, then you could have only one detail line for each order. Other detail records with the same order number would be key violations. Therefore, you must have a second key field in the DETAIL table—which, combined with the Order no., will make each Detail record unique. (Additional items with the same Stock no. should be combined in a single record.) When you have two keys for each detail record, you can use Order no. to link many detail records to a single record in the master table.

Setting Up the Tables

You already have the CUSTOMER table, so you needn't concern yourself about it further. Table 10.1 gives all the details needed to complete the remaining three tables using the File New Table command. When you complete a table, choose Save as, give it the appropriate name, and begin the next table.

Table 10.1
Information for the Order Entry Tables

Field Name	Field Type	Size	Key	Properties
ORDERS Table				
Order no.	N	*		Required Minimum: 100001 Maximum: 999999
Cust. ID	A	5		
Sold by	A	3		Picture: ###
Today's date	D			
Ship via	A	9		Default: Ground Picture: {1-day air, 2-day air, Ground, USPS}
DETAIL Table				
Order no.	N	*		
Stock no.	A	8	*	
Quant	N			
Unit price	$			
INVENTRY Table				
Stock no.	A	8	*	Required Picture: &&-#####
Description	A	40		
Unit price	$			
On hand	N			
Reorder		N		

* Asterisks in the Key column indicate key fields.

Creating the Links

There are three types of links you can create between tables. You can enforce *referential integrity*, which means that:

- No records can exist in a subordinate (child) table that are not linked to a master table.

- Any changes made to either table are automatically reflected in the other.

You can help to ensure that only valid values (those that do not violate referential integrity) are entered by using one table as a *lookup table* for another. Finally, you can create a visual *data model* that links the key fields in your related tables. You'll learn how to create referential integrity and lookup tables now. As noted, you'll create the data model when you design a form in Chapter 11.

Defining Referential Integrity

When you define referential integrity, you create a link between tables so that the value in a given field in a child table *must* exist in the equivalent field in the parent table. In this example, you'll make sure that the order numbers appearing in the DETAIL table exist in the ORDERS table. (This last step isn't strictly necessary if you enter all your data through a form, as you'll learn in Chapter 11. But it will ensure that no data entered independently in the DETAIL table can be invalid.) Follow these quick steps to define a referential integrity relationship.

QUICK STEPS
Defining Referential Integrity

1. Select File Utilities Restructure (or if the table is current, select Table Restructure) and choose the *child* table for which you wish to define referential integrity (in this instance the DETAIL table).

Paradox presents the Restructure dialog box with the field roster.

2. Move to the Table **P**roperties list box in the upper right corner of the window, pull down the list, and select Referential Integrity.

3. Select the **D**efine button.

Paradox displays a dialog box like the one in Figure 10.3.

4. From the **T**able column, choose the *parent* table to which you want to link the current table (in this instance the ORDERS table).

Paradox displays the key fields from the parent table in the Parent's Key area.

5. From the **F**ields column, choose the field(s) that match the key (in this instance Order no.).

Paradox displays the field name(s) in the Child Fields column.

6. Select OK.

7. Enter a name for the referential integrity (Order number) and select OK.

The referential integrity name appears in the box at the right, as shown in Figure 10.4.

8. Select Save.

Now no records can be entered into your DETAIL table that do not contain a valid order number, nor can they refer to any items that don't have an inventory number.

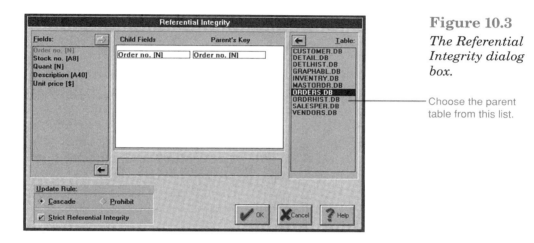

Figure 10.3

The Referential Integrity dialog box.

Choose the parent table from this list.

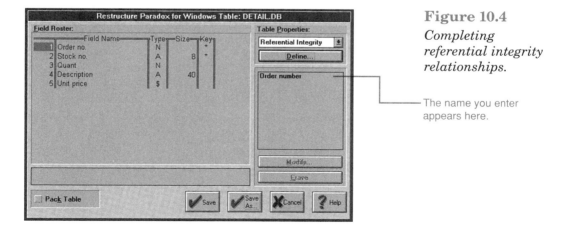

Figure 10.4

Completing referential integrity relationships.

The name you enter appears here.

You may also want to define referential integrity for the ORDERS table, linking it to the CUSTOMER table on the Cust. ID field. This will ensure that you have no orders for customers who aren't in your database.

NOTE: When you define referential integrity, you can link a table only to one other table. To link to additional tables, make them lookup tables.

Linking a Lookup Table

One way to be sure that you don't enter invalid data is to give the user access to the valid data. You do this by letting the user look up the appropriate values in the table where they are stored. In this application, the customers should exist in the CUSTOMER table, and the inventory items in the INVENTRY table. Therefore, both of these tables should be available when taking an order. When you have a lookup table defined, Paradox can automatically copy the correct information from that table to your current table. Follow these Quick Steps to link lookup tables.

Linking a Lookup Table

1. Choose File Utilities Restructure (or if the table is current, choose Table Restructure) and select the child table to which you wish to link a lookup table (in this instance, the DETAIL table).

Paradox presents the Restructure dialog box, with the field roster.

2. Move to the Table **Proper-**ties list box in the upper right corner of the window, pull down the list, and select Table Lookup.

3. Choose the **Define** button.   Paradox displays a dialog box like the one in Figure 10.5.

4. From the **Lookup** Table column, select the table containing the data to be looked up (in this instance INVENTRY).

5. From the **Fields** column, select the field that your current table has in common with the lookup table (in this instance, Stock no.).

6. To allow the user access to all information in the lookup table, select All Corresponding Fields.

7. To have Paradox copy the information to the current table, select Help and Fill.

8. Select OK.

Figure 10.5

Linking a Lookup table.

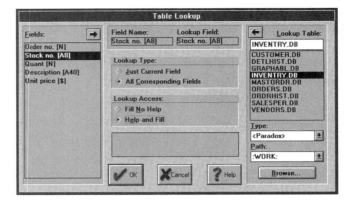

If you want to follow along with the book by creating this application, you'll have to enter at least a few records. Figure 10.6 shows a sample set of records for the INVENTRY table. Enter as few or as many as you wish.

In these records, the Stock no. field contains a five-digit number preceded by a two-letter department code. Because you have entered the value `&&-#####` in the Picture field, you won't have to capitalize the letters. While the table is on the desktop, select the On hand field, and bring up the Object Inspector. Select Number Format Integer. Do the same to the Reorder field.

Note that Stock no. is a key field, and that, following the principles established earlier in this book, the values are arbitrary and unique. The only nonarbitrary part of the stock number is the department code. The five-digit numbers are assigned sequentially within each department.

The Orders Table

Now use File Open Table to bring the ORDERS table to the desktop. This table violates a rule you learned earlier. Notice that the key field is a Numeric, not an Alphanumeric field. Earlier, I suggested that you use numbers only when arithmetic operations would be performed on the values in a field. Since the key value is arbitrary and fixed, why use a number? Because once you learn ObjectPAL, you'll be able to increment the value automatically each time you fill out an order. Unfortunately, the technique is beyond the scope of this book.

```
12/08/92    Standard Report                                          Page 1

Stock no.   Description                     Unit price   On hand   Reorder
--------    ----------------------------    ----------   -------   -------
CF-10023    Printer stand 14" w. fan            489.95        37        12
CF-10024    Printer stand 12" w. fan            439.95        16        10
CF-10025    Printer stand 14"                   439.95        12         8
CF-10026    Printer stand 12"                   389.95         9         8
CO-25438    NoName 286-16 base unit             399.95        62        36
CO-25444    NoName 386DX-33 w. cache base unit  949.95        11        24
CO-25482    NoName 486SX-33 w. 64k cache base unit  1,099.95  31        30
CO-25604    NoName 486DX-50 w. 256k cache base unit 1,449.95  13        30
CO-29817    EZPort 386SX-25 notebook, VGA, 60Mb, 2Mb  1,399.95  43      24
CO-29833    EZPort 486SX-25 notebook, VGA, 80Mb 2Mb   1,999.95  37      24
CP-30571    Perfect Laser PS 4Mb memory       2,989.95        28        24
CP-30614    Perfect Laser 4ppm PCL-4 comp.      649.95        12        24
CP-30622    Perfect Laser 8ppm PCL-5 comp.    1,149.95        14        24
CP-30892    Perfect Printer 24-pin DM std carriage   239.95    38       12
CP-30893    Perfect Printer 24-pin DM wide carriage  329.95    15        8
CS-10210    5 1/4" DSDD Diskettes Standard (10)       4.50   3809     1000
CS-10211    5 1/4" DSDD Diskettes Premium (10)        8.50    880      800
CS-10212    5 1/4" DSHD Diskettes Standard (10)       8.50    512      500
CS-10213    5 1/4" DSHD Diskettes Premium (10)       12.89    963      300
CS-10214    3 1/2" DSDD Diskettes Standard (10)       5.50   1820      800
CS-10215    3 1/2" DSDD Diskettes Premium (10)        9.50    619      500
CS-10216    3 1/2" DSHD Diskettes Standard (10)       9.98    576      300
CS-10217    3 1/2" DSHD Diskettes Premium (10)       13.98    734      300
PP-79868    Roller Pens Fine Black (12)               9.49   1403     1200
PP-79869    Roller Pens Fine Red (12)                 9.49   1543     1200
PP-79870    Roller Pens Fine Blue (12)                9.49   1298     1200
PP-79871    Roller Pens Fine Green (12)               9.49   1233      600
ST-20381    Legal pads yellow 14"                     1.69   6902     7200
ST-20382    Legal pads yellow 11"                     1.39   7891     7200
ST-21919    File folders 1/3 cut letter gross        21.99    421      144
ST-21920    File folders 1/3 cut legal gross         24.99    385      144
ST-23121    Mailing envelopes tyvec 9x12 (12)         6.29    235      144
ST-23122    Mailing envelopes tyvec 10x12 (12)        6.59    311      144
ST-23123    Mailing envelopes tyvec 12x14 (12)        6.99    120      144
ST-38274    Binder 8.5" x 11" x 2"                    4.39   1924     1440
ST-38275    Binder 8.5" x 11" x 1.5"                  3.39   1870     1440
ST-38276    Binder 8.5" x 11" x 1"                    2.39   1683     1440
```

Figure 10.6
A sample inventory database.

The Big Picture

Before proceeding, however, consider the larger business situation into which this little four-table application fits. Obviously, the final orders must go to the Accounts Receivable Department for billing. The items ordered must be subtracted from the inventory.

In turn, the Purchasing Department needs to have the latest inventory figures to maintain the stock. The Accounts Payable Department will need the information from the purchase orders generated by the Purchasing Department. The Shipping Department will need copies of the completed orders—minus pricing information—to pack and ship the orders.

Figure 10.7 shows how the information needed for all these functions can be stored nonredundantly in a relatively small number of tables. (The Shipping Department isn't shown because the information it receives duplicates information found throughout the system.)

Figure 10.7
The flow of information through a database application.

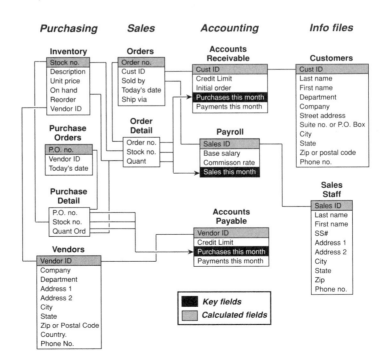

Each box represents a single database table. The three fields indicated by arrows are actually calculated fields, which are derived from the items in the DETAIL tables. I've included them in the diagram so you can see where the information comes from.

The diagram is still not complete. Presumably, the data in the Orders, order detail (Detail), purchase orders (PO), and purchase order detail (PODetl) tables are moved periodically to history files to prevent updating the inventory with the same information more than once.

The last two fields in the Customer database—Credit limit and Initial order—no longer appear in the Customer file. That information is now stored in a file accessible only to the Accounting Department. (Assume that if customers order more than their credit limit allows, the Credit Department will cancel the order. It might be better if the order clerks could do so, but it complicates the picture.)

If you study the diagram carefully, you'll see how it embodies the cardinal rule. Moreover, if you follow the connecting lines, you'll see how all the information needed for any function is available through linking fields.

Other Uses for BLOB Fields

In this chapter, you saw a table containing an inventory of items for sale. You could add a Memo field to a table of this type and use it for an extended description of each item. Moreover, you could use a Graphic field to store pictures of the items in the inventory. You could then use Paradox's reporting function to format this information as catalog copy. Additionally, you could make the data available on-line so that order clerks could give extended information to customers who need to know more than the name of the item.

Creating a New Design Document

1. Choose File New Form (or Report).
2. Select the tables to be used and link them in the Data Model. Click OK.
3. Choose settings in the Design Layout dialog box.
4. Complete the details in the Design window.

Placing a Field in a Form

1. Choose the Field tool.
2. Drag around the area where you want the field to appear.
3. Use the Object Inspector to define the field and select its properties.

11

Creating and Using Design Documents

Paradox includes two types of design documents: forms and reports. You've already been introduced to forms. As you may remember, you can create a quick form for any table by pressing F7, the Quick Form key, or clicking the Quick Form button on the speedbar. You've also been introduced to reports in Chapter 8, where you created a Quick Report based on an ANSWER table. You create Quick Reports by pressing ⇧Shift + F7 or by clicking the Quick Report button on the speedbar.

In principle, the main difference between forms and reports is that forms are designed for viewing and entering data on the screen, while reports are designed for printing on paper. In Paradox for Windows, however, forms and reports are largely interchangeable—you can view your data using a report, or format your data in a form and print it out. In fact, once you've designed your document, you can open a form as a report, and vice versa. Some special characteristics of reports will be discussed at the end of the chapter.

Forms give you alternative views of your data. They allow you to view one record at a time and to see all the fields in a given record at once (if they all fit on one screen).

However, with proper planning, forms can do a great deal more. If set up effectively, a form is especially helpful for both viewing and entering data.

In addition, properly structured forms can allow you to enter data into several tables at once or to view data in linked tables. In this chapter, you'll learn the basics of using Paradox's document design window. Then you'll create and use a form based on a multi-table data model to link the tables in the order-entry application (presented in Chapter 10).

Selecting the Design Layout

We'll begin by designing some forms. As we proceed, I'll point out what would be different if you were designing a report.

To begin designing a form, choose File New Form. (For a report, you'd choose File New Report.) This takes you to the Data Model dialog box, shown in Figure 11.1. To work with a single table, simply choose the table from the list and choose OK. (For this exercise, choose the ROLODEX table.) This takes you immediately to the Design Layout dialog box shown in Figure 11.2.

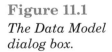

Figure 11.1
*The Data Model
dialog box.*

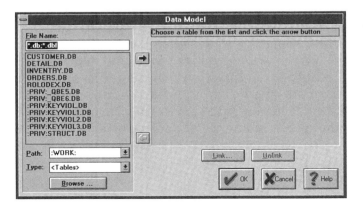

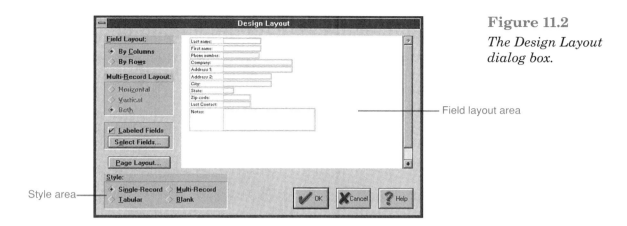

Figure 11.2
The Design Layout dialog box.

Field layout area

Style area

This is only the preliminary design window. With the formatting capabilities built into Windows, you can design a document with virtually any appearance you like, controlling field placement, background colors, and text font, size, style, and color. You can even add graphics created by other applications—a letterhead or company logo, for example. However, if you explore the Design Layout dialog box thoroughly, you'll find that you can make many decisions regarding the appearance of your form before you begin working with the details.

We'll design a form for viewing the ROLODEX table one record at a time and editing the data in it. But first, let's see what options are available.

The large white window gives you a mock-up of your layout. As you can see, each field is represented by a pair of boxes made of dotted lines. The outer box contains the field name and a second box, which shows the location in which the data will appear.

Choosing a Style

Turn your attention to the **S**tyle area at the lower left corner. As you can see, you have a choice of four form styles:

- *Single-Record* displays a single record on a page (or on the screen); this is the default for forms, which you see in Figure 11.2.

- *Multi-Record* displays as many records as will fit, either horizontally, vertically, or both (dividing the screen into four quadrants); you choose the arrangement in the Multi-**R**ecord Layout area, which becomes active when you choose this style.

- *Tabular* creates a table with column headings for each field, in which records appear as rows; this is the default for reports.

- *Blank* clears the screen so that you can individually place fields exactly where you want them.

Now, notice that in the **F**ield Layout area, you can choose to lay out your form By **C**olumns (the default for forms) or By Ro**w**s. When you choose By Ro**w**s, as many fields as will fit are placed on a single line, with the field names above, rather than to the left of, the data areas. When one line is full, the fields continue onto the next line, as shown in Figure 11.3. For this exercise, choose By Rows.

Figure 11.3
*Laying out the
fields in rows.*

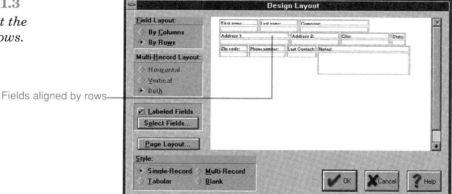

Fields aligned by rows

Choosing a Layout

Turn your attention now to the **P**age Layout button. Choosing this button brings up the Page Layout dialog box. What you see depends on where you started. Figure 11.4 shows the Page Layout dialog box for forms, and Figure 11.5 shows the equivalent for reports. However, if you choose Printer on the form version, you'll have all the same options as for reports, except the margins. Similarly if you choose Screen on the report version, you'll see a screen size and will lose the page formatting options.

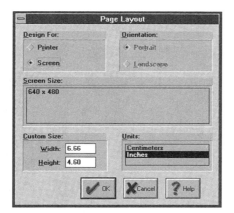

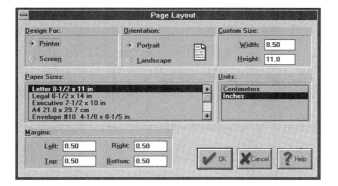

Selecting Fields to Include

Click OK to return to the Design Layout screen. Now choose Select Fields. You'll see a dialog box like the one shown in Figure 11.6. If you had more than one table in your data model, each table would appear in the area to the left with a drop-down list box. The fields in the current table are also shown at the right. If you want to leave some fields out of your form, you can either select them in the Select Fields column and choose Remove Field, or pull down the list box for the table and, using the mouse in combination with ⌂Shift) or Ctrl), deselect one or more fields. If you deselect fields in the left-hand box, they disappear from the right-hand box. If you deselect them in the right-hand box, the highlight disappears from them in the left-hand box.

Figure 11.6
The Select Fields dialog box.

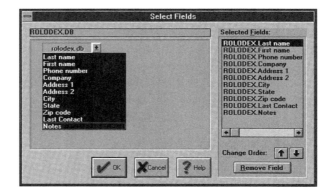

Finally, you can change the order in which the fields appear on the form. To do so, choose the name of the field to move, and use the up arrow or down arrow to move it. For the present form, choose Last name, and move it down so that it appears after First name, and click OK.

The order of the fields as determined in this dialog box has other consequences as well. Normally, you move through a form using Tab⁙), although, as you may remember, the cursor keys also move in various ways through a form. In a custom form, Tab⁙) progresses through the fields in the order in which they appear in this dialog box. When designing forms, you may want to keep this fact in mind. It's easier to enter data in a form if the progression through it matches the order in which the person filling out the form receives the data.

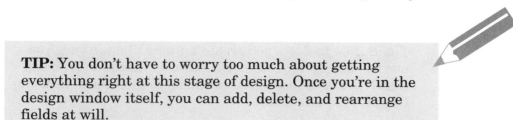

TIP: You don't have to worry too much about getting everything right at this stage of design. Once you're in the design window itself, you can add, delete, and rearrange fields at will.

Working in the Design Window

Now that you've made your selections, click OK. Click OK again in the Design Layout dialog box. Your desktop will display a Form Design window, as shown in Figure 11.7. As you see, you'll have access to a whole new set of menus and speedbar buttons. On the left are the usual Clipboard buttons. The View Data button in the second group takes you out of Design mode and displays your data in the form. Further to the right, you'll see a large group of buttons representing the following design tools:

> The *Selection arrow* lets you select parts of your form or report with which to work. You can select more than one object at a time by holding down Ctrl while clicking on each object to be selected in turn.

> The *Box tool* lets you draw rectangular shapes.

> The *Line tool* lets you draw straight lines.

> The *Ellipse tool* lets you draw circles and ellipses.

> The *Text tool* lets you enter text directly into the form or report design window—text that is not part of any field.

> The *Graphic tool* lets you define an area into which you can import a graphic file via the Clipboard, or directly from another file.

> The *OLE tool* lets you link data from other files to your form or report.

The *Button tool* lets you create buttons like the ones you use in Paradox and other Windows applications. You can attach *methods* (advanced routines) to these buttons using ObjectPAL statements.

The *Field tool* lets you define a new field and place it in your design object.

The *Table tool* lets you place another table—linked or unlinked—in your design document.

The *Multi-record tool* lets you define your design object as a multi-record object; thus, you can override the setting you selected in the Design Layout dialog box.

The *Graph tool* and *Crosstab tool* let you define graphs and crosstabs, respectively, as Chapter 12 will explain.

We'll use quite a few of these tools in this chapter. The rest are beyond the scope of this book.

Figure 11.7

A Design window, showing the Form Design speedbar.

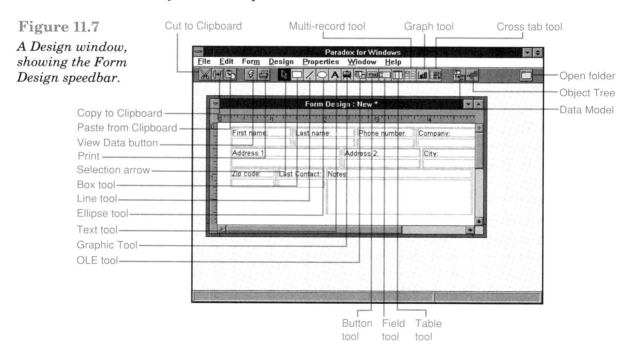

I'd suggest that you maximize the Form Design window so you can see the features clearly. We'll experiment with a few techniques to get comfortable in this window before putting the form into its final arrangement.

Selecting and Deselecting

First, move your mouse pointer around in the window. Notice that its horizontal and vertical position are indicated by lines on the rulers along the borders. If you're designing a screen form in which to enter data to print on pre-printed forms, you can use this fact to position the data entry areas exactly where they need to be to fill in the blanks on the paper.

Next, notice that each field is marked by three dotted rectangles. The outer rectangle contains two others: the field name and the data area. You can select any of these three objects for manipulation. Click on the First name field, and you'll see a set of "handles" appear around the outer box, as shown in Figure 11.8. These handles appear whenever you select an object. You can use them to stretch or shrink the selected object(s) much as you would use the border of a window. When an object is selected, its dimensions and position are indicated on the ruler by a shaded area.

To select the field name (the *label area*), click in it while the outer border is selected. You'll see the heavy border containing the handles move to this area. Similarly, you can select the data area of a field by first selecting the entire field area, then double-clicking in the data area.

To select multiple objects, hold down the Ctrl key while selecting. For example, hold down Ctrl and click in the First name field. Release the mouse button, but keep the Ctrl key depressed. Click on the Last name field. As you'll see from the highlight on the border, both fields are now selected. To deselect any one of several selected objects, click it while pressing the Ctrl key. The other objects will remain selected.

Figure 11.8
Selecting a field.

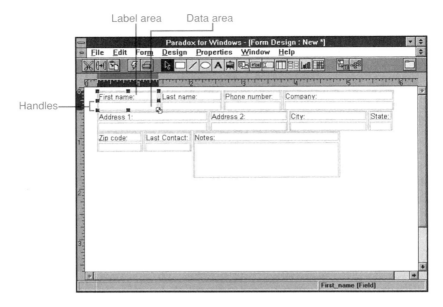

You can select any number of objects and manipulate them as a group (something you'll learn about shortly), or you can change the properties of all the objects in the group at once. Try selecting and deselecting a variety of objects. As you do, notice the effect on the highlight on the rulers. (Note that you can't select more than one object at a time using the keyboard.)

NOTE: When you want to select *part* of several objects, you must double-click in the parts you want to select after you've selected the first one. Clicking once deselects the containing object.

TIP: When several objects are selected, clicking on any one object without pressing Ctrl deselects all the other selected objects and selects the object on which you clicked.

NOTE: The entire "page" itself is an object. Click outside any of the existing objects, and you'll see the highlight cover the entire ruler; handles will appear at the margins.

You can also select any item on the screen using Tab↹ and ⇧Shift+Tab↹. The Tab↹ key moves to the entire field, the label area, and the data area in turn, then moves on to the next field. If you wish, you can add more pages to a form by choosing Form Page Add.

Using the Size Handles

As noted, the handles let you resize an object. You'll find, however, that you can't make an object any smaller than its initial size. It has to be large enough to hold the amount of data specified when you created the table.

You might decide that the Notes field would be more useful if it were larger. To enlarge it, select the field. When you see the handles, drag the bottom center one downward to enlarge the field. You'll find that you've enlarged only the frame, not the data area. To enlarge the data area, double-click in it while the entire field is selected. The handles will move to the inner box. Drag the lower border downward until it fills the area inside the outer box.

TIP: You can add a vertical scroll bar to the Notes field or to any field that might contain more text than will fit in the allotted space.

Moving Objects in the Design Window

Once an object is selected, you can move it to anywhere you want by placing the mouse pointer on it, clicking, and dragging it to its desired location. If several objects are selected, they will all move together. Select the Last contact and Notes fields, and drag them toward the bottom of the window. This will make room for you to arrange your fields more logically. We'll do that now. We'll set up the fields so that the name appears on the first line, followed by the phone number on the second, a properly formatted address, and the incidental information. You'll be aiming for an arrangement something like the one in Figure 11.9. Granted, it's rather messy, but you'll clean it up shortly using the commands on the **D**esign menu, shown in Figure 11.10.

TIP: If you don't have enough room for some of the fields, select all the ones below the space you want to move using `Ctrl` and the left mouse button, and drag them out of the way.

Figure 11.9

Arranging fields by hand.

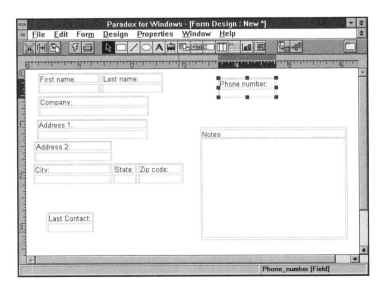

Figure 11.10
The Design menu.

Using the Design Menu

The **D**esign menu lets you manipulate the *relationship* among the design objects in your window, as opposed to their individual properties. Notice that if you need to return to the Design Layout dialog box, you can do so from here.

Aligning Objects

Your form would look better if the objects in each row were aligned properly. Begin by selecting the three fields on the first line (First name, Last name, and Phone number) by using Ctrl and the left mouse button, then choose **D**esign **A**lign Align **T**op. Now do the same with the City, State, and Zip code fields.

Now, it would be nice if you could select all the fields along the left border and align them. But if you just select the leftmost fields, Last name, State, and Zip code won't move along with them. And if you select these three fields as well, they will be moved to the left along with everything else, so that the several fields on a single line will be on top of one another. This isn't what you want. However, there is a solution—grouping.

TIP: Notice that the **A**lign submenu is divided into two sections. The commands in the upper section align objects along a horizontal axis, while those in the lower section align objects along a vertical axis. This fact will help you to remember the difference between Align **M**iddle, which centers the objects vertically, and Align **C**enter, which centers them horizontally. If you select a group of objects that are next to each other and choose Align **C**enter, they'll all be stacked together, one on top of the next, and you won't be able to read them.

Working with Groups

When you *group* several objects, the group is then (for many purposes) treated as a single object. This lets you maintain the arrangement of several objects relative to each other while changing the relationship of that group to other objects.

Select First name and Last name and choose Design Group. You'll see the outer box change to encompass both label areas and data areas, while the handles rearrange themselves to reflect the fact that these fields now form a single object. Do the same to the City, State, and Zip code fields. Now you can safely select all the fields along the left side of the screen and use the Design Align Align Left command. Now select the Phone number and Notes fields, and repeat the procedure. They'll move to a common left margin without altering their vertical relationship.

CAUTION   Selecting works differently on grouped objects. If you try to select an area contained within the group border, you'll select the group itself. You can still select any object within the group by positioning the mouse pointer carefully before clicking. If you want to select objects that are part of several groups, such as those in your address area, you may have to *double-click* on them, as clicking once will simply deselect them.

Creating and Using Graphic Objects

As noted, the speedbar contains a set of rather primitive drawing tools. However, you can do quite a bit with them. With lines, ellipses, boxes, and text, you may have all the materials you need to design company logos, holiday designs, special symbols representing company functions, and so on. Remember that every object you create can have properties such as colors, patterns, and borders. Text can be styled with all the standard Windows text properties. However, once you've made a design that you like, you'll need to keep it together by selecting the parts and grouping them. You can then place your completed design anywhere in your design window.

You may also find the **D**esign Bring to **F**ront and **D**esign Send to **B**ack commands essential for keeping your design elements in their proper order. You might lay an ellipse over a box, for example, and then decide that because the box bisects the ellipse you want to change the order.

The example shown here was created with an ellipse, a rectangle, and a text box.

Adjusting Spacing

Because you were dragging your fields freehand, they may not be evenly spaced on the screen. Your form will be attractive if all the fields in the upper left portion—the name and address fields—are evenly spaced. To ensure that they are, deselect the Last contact field and choose Design Adjust Spacing Vertical. (You can use the Horizontal command to adjust the spacing of fields that are arrayed across the window.) Your finished form should now look something like Figure 11.11.

TIP: You might want to group all the fields that make up your address area. That way, they will maintain their relationship when you edit the form further, and you won't have to keep aligning them. In general, it's a good idea to group any items whose spatial relationship shouldn't change.

Figure 11.11

A first draft for a Rolodex form.

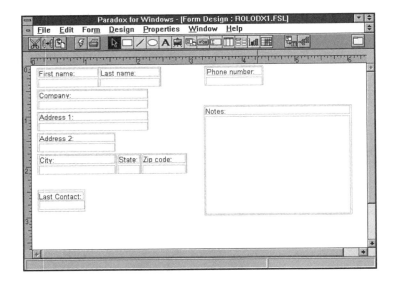

Saving Your Work

Before you go any further, pull down the File menu. You'll see that, for the first time, the Save and Save as commands are available. These commands are available only in document design windows. (When you edit a table, a record is saved as soon as the cursor leaves it, so it isn't necessary to save a table file.) The Save command is used to save a design document, while the Save as command lets you make a second copy of it with a new name. Since you haven't yet given this document a name, you can use either command. Give the form the name `rolodex1`. Paradox will supply the appropriate file extension.

NOTE: When you close a document design window, Paradox will ask if you want to save it (if you haven't already), or if you've made changes since the last time you saved the file. You should save design documents frequently, so that you don't lose your work if something goes wrong with your system.

Testing the Result

Click the View Data button to see how your new form works with the data in your table. It should look something like Figure 11.12. Not so good, is it? The main problem is that field labels and field data are displayed exactly the same way. This makes it hard to pick out the data from among the rest of the information on the screen.

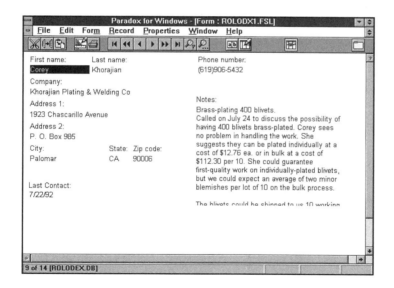

Figure 11.12
Viewing your data in the form.

Working with Properties

There are several ways you can change the form, any or all of which might improve the results. All involve working with the Object Inspector, the menu which you see in Figure 11.13. (You can reach this menu by choosing Properties Current Object, clicking the right mouse button, or pressing F6.)

Figure 11.13

The Object Inspector menu.

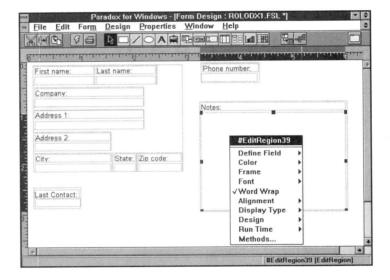

Here are some ways you might improve the form:

- Select the label area of all fields and use a different font, style, size, or color, or a combination of these attributes.

- Select the data area of all fields and change the background color so that the fields are visible even when empty.

- Select the data area of all fields and add a border to all of them.

- Go back to the Design Layout dialog box, and uncheck Labeled Fields, so all you see is the data. (This may be an adequate solution for viewing data, but won't be very helpful if you want to enter or edit data.)

We'll apply a few of these improvements to the present form, and several of them to various design documents in the course of this chapter. Before we begin, however, let's study this menu, because some of it is rather cryptic.

Name appears at the top, highlighted. It is the *name* of the object. Every object except a group has a name. You can change the name of any object by clicking on its name. This may be useful if you program in ObjectPAL, because you can refer to objects by name.

Define Field lets you see a list of the fields in your table, with the current field checked. Later in the chapter, you'll use this item to define fields that don't exist in your table.

Color, *Frame*, *Font*, and *Alignment* all perform their expected functions, and may be used for styling the objects in your form or report.

Word Wrap is a toggle which may be used to allow the data in a field to occupy more than one line. By default, Memo and Formatted memo fields are word-wrapped, while other types of fields aren't.

Methods are ObjectPAL routines, a subject beyond the scope of this book. The remaining items deserve a bit more explanation.

Display Type lets you create objects of various types that mimic the functions of standard Windows programs:

- *Labeled* adds the field name to the form or report; if you left **L**abeled fields checked in the design document window, this will be the default.

- *Unlabeled* lets you remove the field label.

- *Drop-Down Edit* lets you turn a field into a drop-down list box, from which the user can choose one alternative. This is quite useful when a field accepts only one of a limited number of values. We'll use this selection later in the chapter.

- *Radio Buttons* and *Check Boxes* are also useful for dealing with a limited number of choices. Using these items successfully, however, involves defining new fields and/or attaching ObjectPAL methods to the objects.

Finally, *Run Time* determines several aspects of the way a field is treated while you are entering or editing data in the form:

- *Visible* (the default) is a toggle that determines whether the object can be seen in your design document. There are times when you'll want to hide an object, as you'll see later in this chapter.

- *Read Only*, when checked, prevents the field from being edited. This is especially useful when you want to include a lookup table directly in your design document, but don't want the user to be able to alter the values within it.

- *Tab Stop* ensures that `Tab ⇥` and the cursor keys will enter the field during editing. Deselecting this item effectively makes the field a read-only field.

- *No Echo* allows the data to appear in the field. If you select this item, the check mark will disappear, and thereafter, the field will appear to be blank. This is useful for such items as passwords.

If you select the frame containing both the label area and the data area, you also get two more options:

- *Horizontal Scroll Bar* lets you add a horizontal scroll bar to a field.

- *Vertical Scroll Bar* lets you add a vertical scroll bar to a field.

TIP: If a field is of the Date, Numeric, or Currency type, you can also select Format, and choose a numeric or date format for the field. If the field is in an embedded table, you can choose its format by first selecting the field definition in the first record, then bringing up the Object Inspector.

Styling a Form or Report

Now that you know what's in the arsenal, let's use some of these tools to make the form more legible. As you've probably noticed, the View Data icon on the speedbar changed to a Design icon (see Figure 11.14) when the window became a viewing window. Click that icon, or choose Form Design or press F8 to bring back the design window.

Our first step will be to assign different fonts to the label areas and the data areas. There are two ways to proceed.

- Select a single label area, then display the Object Inspector menu by one of the three means described. Choose Font, and click the thumbtack. You can then choose a font, style, and size for the selected label; you can move to each label area in turn, repeating this procedure. The Font dialog box will remain open until you close it by clicking the thumbtack again.

- Hold down Ctrl and select *all* the label areas. (You may not be able to select some if they are grouped.) Open the Object Inspector while pointing to one of the label areas. Choose Font. Click the thumbtack. Choose a font, size, and style to be applied to all the label areas.

The second approach is probably quicker. If you can't select some of the label areas, go back and select them individually before you close the Font dialog box.

Now click anywhere in the window to deselect the label areas and select the data areas. Press F6, or use one of the other means to bring up the Object Inspector, and choose Color. Choose a light color. You'll see it applied to all the data areas. Repeat the procedure. While the data areas are still selected, choose Frame, and pick a frame style. When you're finished, you should have a form resembling Figure 11.14. Quite an improvement, isn't it?

TIP: If you can't see all of the frame around some areas, enlarge the gray box containing both the data area and the label area: select it and drag the lower border downward slightly.

Figure 11.14
A fully styled form.

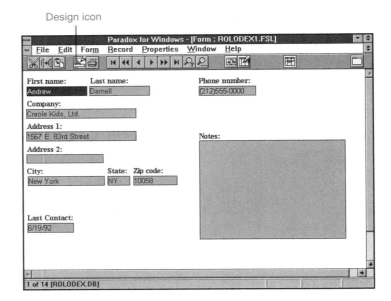

Designing Multi-Table Forms and Reports

In this section, we'll use the tables presented in Chapter 10 to create an order-entry form. This will look very much like an invoice on the screen.

Designing the Data Model

The first step in designing a multi-table form or report is to design the data model. To do that, you first select the tables to include in the form, and then link them. I'll go over this procedure step-by-step, because it's tricky.

The first step is a logical one. If you have defined referential integrity for any of your tables, that information will automatically be used when you create the links. A referential integrity relationship automatically implies a *one-to-many* relationship between the parent table and the child table. In other words, for every record in the parent table, the form will contain a tabular area displaying the child records (although, of course, you can change that).

Let's think about our multi-table order-entry application. We defined referential integrity between the CUSTOMER and ORDERS tables, with the ORDERS table as the child. Similarly, we defined referential integrity between the ORDERS and DETAIL tables, with DETAIL as the child. This is perfectly logical, since one customer can have many orders, and one order can have many detail records.

However, we have a problem here. Because of the way links are created in the data model, this arrangement will result in a form in which the CUSTOMER table is the parent, and detail tables will appear for both orders and details of the orders. This isn't what an invoice should look like. Therefore, although ORDERS is logically a child of CUSTOMER, we must *remove* the referential integrity relationship between these two tables and trust that the data model will keep the relationship intact. So if you're going to create this form, before you begin, take the following steps.

1. Choose File Table Utilities Restructure.

2. Select the ORDERS table.

3. In the Table **P**roperties list box, choose Referential Integrity.

4. Choose Erase.

5. Choose Save.

Now you're ready to design the invoice. Follow these steps.

1. Choose File New Form. You'll see the Data Model dialog box, shown in Figure 11.15.

Figure 11.15
Designing a multi-table data model.

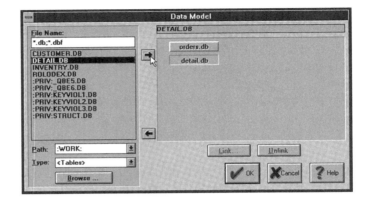

2. Select ORDERS.DB, and click →. You'll see the highlight and the table name disappear from the list box.

3. Repeat step 2 with DETAIL.DB, CUSTOMER.DB, and INVENTRY.DB.

4. Now you're ready to define the links. In the central area, click the ORDERS.DB button, and drag to the DETAIL.DB button. You'll see a gray line stretch from one to the other, followed by an illustration of a link forming between two tables, as shown in Figure 11.16. When you release the mouse button, you'll see a double-headed arrow pointing from ORDERS.DB to DETAIL.DB. The double-headed arrow indicates that a referential integrity relationship exists between these tables.

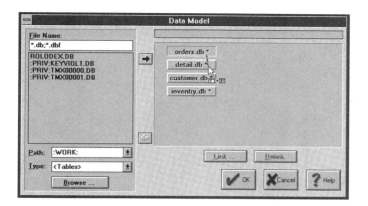

Figure 11.16
Creating a link in a data model.

5. Click the ORDERS.DB button again and drag to the CUSTOMER.DB button. You'll be taken to the Define Link dialog box, shown in Figure 11.17. In the **F**ields box, choose Cust.ID, the only field the two tables have in common. Double-click it, or click the →, and you'll see the field name appear in both columns in the center box. Choose OK.

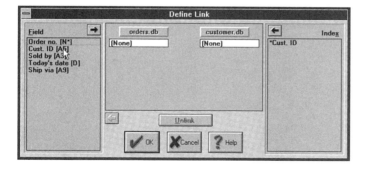

Figure 11.17
Defining a link between tables.

6. You'll now be back in the Data Model dialog box, and the central area will contain a diagram showing how the tables are linked. Notice (see Figure 11.18) that the arrow to the CUSTOMER table has only one head, indicating that it's linked only through the data model, not by referential integrity. Choose OK and you'll find yourself at the Design Layout screen.

Figure 11.18
The completed data model.

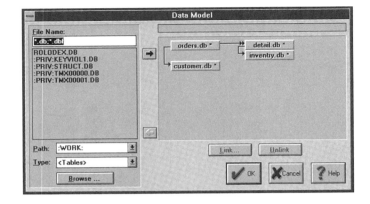

7. In the **O**bject Layout section, choose By Rows. As you'll see in Figure 11.19, you now have something resembling a proper invoice form.

Figure 11.19
Design Layout for an invoice form.

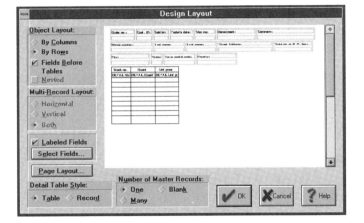

8. There's only one more small refinement. Click the Select Fields button. In the list at the right of the Select Field dialog box, choose CUSTOMER:Credit Limit and click Remove field. Repeat the procedure for CUSTOMER: Initial Order. Choose OK.

9. When you're back at the Design Layout dialog box, choose OK again. This will take you to the design window. From

here, you know how to proceed. See if you can duplicate the form shown in Figure 11.20. Notice that the Ship via field is a drop-down list. To make it look like the illustration, you have to make the field Unlabeled, then use the Text tool to add the text for the label directly to the form. Otherwise the list box will be the size of the containing frame.

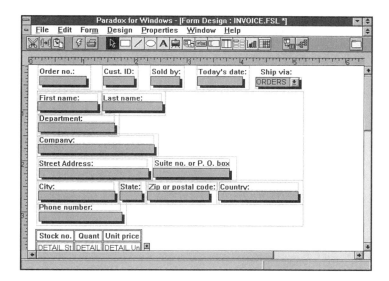

Figure 11.20
The basic design of an invoice form.

Working with Embedded Tables

The fields that appear in embedded tables have a few different properties from those fields that appear individually (as in the upper portion of our form):

- As with data tables, you can adjust the size of any column by dragging its right border.

- As with data tables, you can reorder the columns by selecting the column to move and dragging it to the left or right.

- You can adjust the number of records visible in the entire table by dragging the handle on the lower border of the frame upwards or downwards.

- From the Object Inspector, you can detach the header from the data lines.

- From the Object Inspector, you can define the details of the table grid, including such refinements as whether the records are separated by a line.

Creating Calculated and Summary Fields

We're not quite finished, however. We need to try something a little more adventurous. The table portion needs a column for the price extension, and the entire form needs a field in which to display the total cost of the order, so that the order clerk can read the information back to the customer.

Creating a New Field in a Table

To create a new column in the table, follow these Quick Steps.

Creating a New Field in a Table	
1. Select the table.	
2. Double-click in a single column, until that column is highlighted.	
3. Press Ins.	Paradox creates a new column, with the heading LABEL, and the field definition Undefined Field, as shown in Figure 11.21.

NOTE: I also reduced the number of records visible in the table by dragging upward on the lower handle, and added a scroll bar on the right so you can see additional detail lines if necessary.

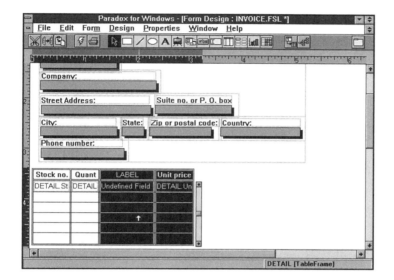

Figure 11.21
Adding a column to a table in a form.

Now that you've created your new field, you must define it. But first, select it by double-clicking, then drag it to the right, so that it becomes the rightmost column. This is the correct position for the extension. Select the header, delete LABEL, and type in `Extension`.

Defining a Calculated Field

To define a calculated field, you must first select it. Click on the text Undefined Field, and you'll see a list of fields. At the top of the list will be either three dots or the text More fields...; choose that, and you'll go to the Define Field Object dialog box. Since you're defining a calculated field, check the Calculated box.

The basic principles of defining a calculated field are the same as those of defining a calculation in a query. The main difference is that you refer to the data in existing fields not by example elements (which are not available) but by their field names in brackets. In theory, the calculation you want to enter is

```
Quant * Unit price
```

but you must give Paradox enough information to be able to identify the field fully. The easiest way to do this is to select the field to be entered into the calculation from the drop-down list attached to the table name, as shown in Figure 11.22. Then choose Copy Field. The field name (including the name of the table in which the field is found) moves to the edit line. The field name will be highlighted, so you must press → before you enter anything else in the edit line. Otherwise, the field name you have so laboriously placed there will disappear.

Figure 11.22
Setting up a calculation.

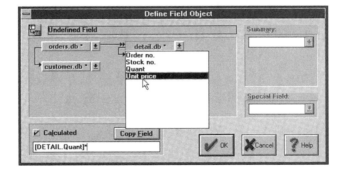

Follow these Quick Steps to create a calculated field for the extension.

Defining a Calculated Field

1. Click the right mouse button to bring up the Object Inspector.

Paradox displays the Object Inspector menu.

2. Click on the field name, which will have the form `#Field`*nnn*. Give the field an appropriate name (`Extension`) and choose OK.

3. Bring up the inspector again, and choose Define Field.

Paradox displays a list of the fields in the form. At the top will be either three dots, or the text `More Fields....`

4. Choose the topmost item in the list.

Paradox displays the Define Field window with the Data Model diagram in the center.

5. Check Calculated.

6. If your calculation is based on values contained in other fields, pull down the list box attached to the appropriate table name (in this case, DETAIL.DB). Choose Copy Field.

The field name moves to the edit line.

7. Repeat step 6 for any other fields to be included in the application.

continues

continued

8. Add any operators, constants, and separators needed to complete the formula.

9. Choose OK.
Paradox returns you to the Design Window, with the text `Undefined Field` changed to `formula`.

Now that you've got your calculated field, select it, bring up the Object Inspector, and turn off Screen Font. You don't want someone trying to change the results of the calculation. While you're at it, you might turn off Tab Stop as well.

Altering the Data Model

Since you've made INVENTRY a lookup table for the detail records, these fields will be filled directly from that table. To make that possible, you have to add the INVENTRY table to the data model. Click the Data Model button on the speedbar to bring back the Data Model dialog box. Choose inventry.db, and move it to the center area. Drag from detail.db to inventry.db to create the link.

Now you must add yet another column to the table. Double-click the Quant column and press Ins. Use the Object Inspector and choose Define Field. Select INVENTRY:Description from the list. You'll see the label at the top of the column change to `Description`. You'll want to widen the column, and style the label to match the others. When you've done that, bring up the Object Inspector, choose Run Time, and uncheck Tab Stop. (Since you won't be able to edit this field, there's no point allowing the cursor to go to it.)

Using Multi-Table Forms

Now that your form is complete, use it to enter a few records to see how it works. You can do one of three things:

- Press F9 (the Edit Data key).
- Click the View Data button on the speedbar and press F9.
- Choose Form Edit Data.

You'll see a highlight in the first field. Type 100001 and press Tab⇵. Now you'll be in the Cust. ID field. You've linked the CUSTOMER table to this field as a lookup table, so press Ctrl+Spacebar to access it. This displays the lookup table in a dialog box, as shown in Figure 11.23. You can scroll through this box to find the information you need, but the linking field (in this case, Cust.ID), remains on the screen. When you've found the appropriate record, press ⏎Enter or choose OK, and all the pertinent information about the customer will be transferred to your form.

Fill in an appropriate Sales ID (a three-digit number) and today's date. Now move to the Ship via field and choose a shipping method. You can either press ← and → to cycle through the selections, or click on the arrow and choose one from the list.

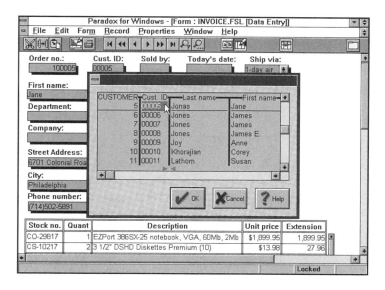

Figure 11.23
Using a LOOKUP table.

Now you're ready to select the items to be ordered. There are three ways to move to the embedded table:

- Keep pressing `Tab⇕` to move through all the fields to the first field of the first detail record.

- Press `F3`.

- Press `F4`.

Pressing `F3` and `F4` moves the cursor among all the tables in a data model. The only difference is that `F3` moves to the last field of the previous table, and `F4` moves to the first field.

When you're in the Stock no. field, you should be able to access the INVENTRY table as a lookup table by pressing `Ctrl`+`Spacebar`, just as you did with the CUSTOMER table. Enter a value in the Quant column and you've completed a detail record. You should see the extension appear as soon as you enter the quantity. The `Tab⇕` key will move you through the first two columns of the embedded table, because you've turned off Tab Stop for all the others.

To move to the next record when you're finished, you can either:

- Press `PgDn`

  or

- Click the right-arrow button on the speedbar.

If you try to continue with `Tab⇕`, you'll find you can move only to the first empty record in the detail table.

Attaching a Design Document to a Query

There are times when you need to create a report to show the results of a query. If this is a procedure you have to repeat, you can simplify it by attaching the design document to the query. Then you don't have to create it each time you need the report.

To do this, first create the query and save it. Next, when you create your design document, go to the **T**ype drop-down list and choose <Queries> instead of <Tables>. You can then proceed as you would with any other design document. When you need to update the report, run the query and choose File Open Report (or Form) to see the latest results.

Special Features of Reports

Reports, as you know, are similar to forms, but are designed primarily for the printer rather than the screen. Two features differentiate them further: *bands* and *grouping*. Bands control when and how parts of reports are repeated. Grouping organizes the records according to criteria you specify.

You'll get a look at both of these tools. You'll use bands to set up a series of mailing labels. Then you'll use the grouping feature to create a report that groups your customers by Zip code.

Mailing Labels

To set up a report to print mailing labels from your customer database, follow these steps:

1. Choose File New Report or right-click the Report button on the speedbar and choose New.

2. Select customer.db and choose OK. You'll be in the Design Layout dialog box.

3. Choose Page Layout and set all four margins to 0. Choose OK to close the dialog box.

4. In the **S**tyle area, choose Multi-Record.

5. Uncheck Labeled.

6. In the Multi-**R**ecord Layout area, choose **B**oth.

7. If you want 3-up labels, choose By Columns in the **F**ield Layout area. If you want 2-up labels, choose By Rows in the **F**ield Layout area.

8. Choose Select Fields and remove the following fields:

First Name

Last Name

City

State

Zip or postal code

Credit limit

Initial order

The easiest way to do this is to pull down the list box at the left, hold down Ctrl, and click on each of the fields. Choose OK. At this point, your Design Layout window should look like Figure 11.24 (assuming you're using 3-up labels). As you can see, Paradox arranges the records in rows across the page. Choose OK. You'll notice that the Report speedbar includes several new icons.

Figure 11.24
Design Layout for mailing labels.

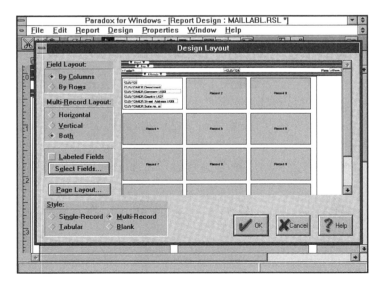

Combining Alphanumeric Fields

I'm sure you're wondering why you eliminated so many essential fields. How can mail be delivered without an addressee or location? Well, you're going to put that information back and learn a new technique in the process—combining, or *concatenating*, alphanumeric fields.

First, rearrange the fields so that they match Figure 11.25. (You'll notice that when you use unlabeled fields, the field name appears within the data area. If you can't read the entire name, select the field, and the name will appear on the status line.) The Cust. ID field should be at the upper right corner, and it's all right for the Street Address and Suite no. fields to overlap—they'll fit properly on the page once the data appears. At this point, it might be a good idea to save the file. Call it `maillabl`.

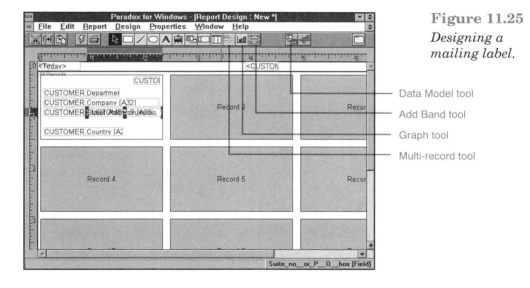

Figure 11.25
Designing a mailing label.

Now choose the Field tool from the speedbar. Place a new field at the upper left and aligned at the left with the existing fields. Now follow these steps:

1. Open the Object Inspector, and choose Display Type Unlabeled.

2. Open the Object Inspector again. Choose Define Field. Choose the three dots at the top of the list to open the Define Field Object dialog box.

3. Check Calculated.

4. Pull down the customer.db list box, select First name, and choose Copy Field.

5. Press ⬇ to remove the highlight, and type +" "+ (a plus sign, a quotation mark, a space, another quotation mark, and another plus sign). This tells Paradox to treat the space character as a literal value.

6. Pull down the customer.db list box, select Last name, and choose Copy Field.

7. Choose OK.

What you've just done is to tell Paradox to take whatever value appears in the First name field, add a space to it, and append the contents of the Last name field. This creates a much neater address than simply placing the two fields on the first line, which would leave a large space between the names.

Next, you'll perform a similar operation on the City, State, and Zip or Postal code fields.

Again use the Field tool to create a field, this time in the blank line near the bottom. Make it an unlabeled field. Now use the Object Inspector to get to the Define Field Object dialog box and take the following steps:

1. Check Calculated.

2. Pull down the customer.db list box, select City, and choose Copy Field.

3. Press ⬇ to remove the highlight, and type +", "+. (Note that the comma goes *inside* the quote marks.)

4. Pull down the customer.db list box, select State, and choose Copy Field.

5. Press ⇥ to remove the highlight, and type +" "+.

6. Pull down the customer.db list box, select Zip or postal code, and choose Copy Field.

7. Choose OK.

You're now almost ready to check your work. One peculiarity of reports is that every record, and various other objects, has a frame around it by default. Select the entire page. Open the Object Inspector and choose Frame. Select the blank rectangle with no frame. Do the same to the first record in the upper left corner. Now press F8, click the View Data button, or choose Report Preview. Soon you should see your file set up to print as mailing labels, as shown in Figure 11.26.

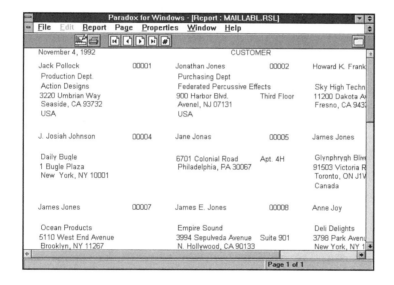

Figure 11.26
Mailing labels ready to print.

What Bands Do

You may have noticed the horizontal bands in the Design Layout window in Figure 11.23. You don't see them on your screen when you use the Design or View Data windows. But they are present. To make them stand out, click the Design button on the speedbar (or choose Report Design) and choose Properties Band Labels.

You should now see the bands, as shown in Figure 11.27. Bands are indicated by their name on a horizontal line. A small downward-pointing triangle indicates the margin of a band at the top of a page, and a similar upward-pointing triangle indicates the lower margin of a band.

Figure 11.27

Displaying the report bands.

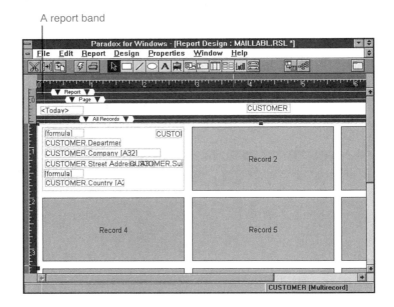

If you scroll to the bottom of the window, you'll see matching bands at the bottom, in reverse order, with the pointers pointing upward.

Each band is contained within the next. The All Records band is at the center and is set within the Page band, which includes a standard header consisting of the system date, the table name, and a page number. The space between the All Records band at the top of the page and the Page band is the *page header band*. The similar space at the bottom is the *page footer band*.

The page band is contained within the Report band, which is marked at the top and bottom of the window.

Although there is no space between the Page band and the Report band, you can make some by selecting the Page band ruler and dragging it downward. In this space, you can include any information that should appear only at the beginning of the entire report. Similarly, you can create a report footer band at the bottom to contain only information to appear at the end. Any material in the page header band appears at the top of every page, and any material in the page footer band appears at the bottom of every page.

Since this report will be used to print mailing labels, you don't want anything in the header or footer bands; in fact, you don't need such bands at all. But you can't get rid of them. What you can do is select and delete each of the fields in the page header band, and then drag the upper margin of the Page band right down to the All Fields band margin. If you don't, there will be a line space at the top and bottom of the label page, which may throw your labels out of line. (If you do a test print and find that your labels are creeping up the page, you may be able to fix the alignment by putting this space back in.)

NOTE: You cannot move bands with the keyboard.

Grouping Records

Suppose your mailing list was much larger than our sample, and you wanted to prepare a mass mailing. The Postal Service requires that mass mailings be grouped by Zip code. You can arrange for this by adding a *group band* to your report.

You'll want to group the records, not the pages or the report itself. A group band must be placed *just outside* the band it groups. Therefore, to group all your records by Zip code, you must first select the All Records band. Next, choose Report Add Band. This displays the Define Group dialog box shown in Figure 11.28. Select the field on which to group your records as shown. You'll notice that you can also group your records in sets of a given number of records, or group those that fall into a given range. When you choose OK, you'll see that a band called Group Records on CUSTOMER.DB:Zip or postal code has appeared inside the Page band (see Figure 11.29). Paradox has kindly placed a labeled field in the band header, with a data area so that you can see what the band represents when you view your report.

Figure 11.28
The Define Group dialog box.

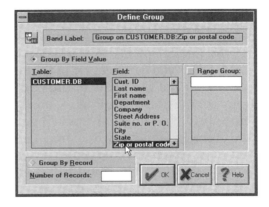

Figure 11.29
Adding a group band.

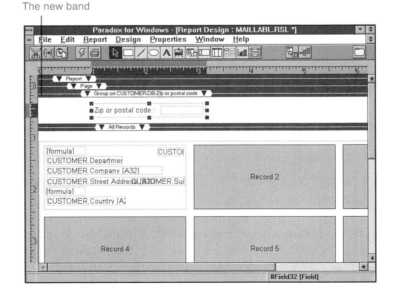

You can add any information you need to a group band using the Text tool or add fields using the Field tool, but for mailing labels, you can simply delete the field and move the group band up to the Page band.

If you wanted to see which customers were in each state, you might add a band grouping the records by the State field between the Zip or postal code band and the Page band.

TIP: You can place summary fields in the header or footer of any band. They will reflect summary values for all the values in each group represented by the band.

Opening a Form as a Report and Vice Versa

If you've designed a form that you like, you can use it as a report, and vice versa. In the Open Document dialog box, choose Open As and select the type of document you want from the drop-down list.

Be aware that there are differences between forms and reports. If you were to open your ROLODEX1 form as a report, for example, you would not find page breaks at the end of each record. Rather, the next record would continue on the same page, and the page break would fall arbitrarily. You can, however, insert a page break wherever you want in a report by clicking in the vertical ruler.

On the other hand, you lose some information when you open a report as a form. Any items that reside outside the record band will not appear in the form, and summaries may behave differently. However, when you open a design document as something it's not, Paradox regards it as a new design document. You can go into the Design window and fine-tune the details so that it works.

Printing

You can print your design document to see how it looks by choosing **File Print** when the Design window is open. To print a report, first make sure that you're in View mode, so that you can see a preview. If everything appears as you want it to, choose **File Print**, and Paradox will print the report exactly as you see it on the screen.

You can print forms with data in them as well.

Creating a Summary Calculated Field

You may have noticed that our invoice has no place for a grand total—in fact, it's impossible to create one given the materials we're working with. But there's a solution. It's tricky, and the details are too complex for this book, but here are the basic priciples:

1. Add a calculated field to one of the source tables (in this instance, add the Extension filed as a currency field to the DETAIL table).

2. Create a query based on that table, in which the Extension filed contains a CALC formula multiplying Quant by Unit price. Run the query once.

3. Add the query to the data model.

4. In place of the calculated field in the form you've worked with, use the new Extension field from the query table (in your data model it will have the name of the calculation, not the name of the field).

5. Below the tabular area, create a field with the Field tool. Define it as a calculated field, and give it the definition

Sum([Quant * Unit price])

Creating Quick Graphs

1. Select the table containing the items to be
   graphed.
2. Press Ctrl+F7, click on the Quick Graph
   button on the speedbar, or choose Table Quick
   Graph.
3. Select the field for the X-axis values from the
   table's drop-down list of fields.
4. Select the Graph Type.
5. Select the field(s) for the Y-axis values from the
   table's drop-down list of fields.
6. If the graph is a summary graph, select the type
   of summary from the Summary list.
7. Choose OK.
8. Open the Object Inspector to select the Graph
   Type.
9. Add styling as desired by opening the Object
   Inspector on various parts of the graph.

Graphs and Crosstabs

You have learned how to view data on the screen in a form designed for that purpose and how to create printed reports. In the process, you've learned ways to link tables in order to gather the data to place into your forms and reports.

Paradox for Windows gives you two more ways of viewing your data:

- Graphs

- Cross-tabulated tables

Paradox's graphing component allows you any degree of control and complexity you like. If your table is properly set up, you can get a simple graph just by clicking on the Quick Graph button on the speedbar, pressing Ctrl+F7, or choosing Table Quick Graph when a table window is open.

On the other hand, you can customize your graphs to your heart's content. Paradox's graphing menus allow you to choose from 17 types of graphs. You can customize the colors (for printing and for viewing on the proper equipment), the fill patterns, the titles and legends, the typefaces and all other aspects of the fonts used, and many other details of the graph's appearance. But you can get usable graphs just by accepting the defaults.

Cross-tabulated tables, or crosstabs, are rather like spread-sheets. The data in the columns is broken down into categories based on the items in the row labels. But because a database table doesn't really have row labels—just record numbers—you have to create this special type of table to provide the information from which to create certain types of graphs.

How Paradox Selects Items to Graph

The most important issue in graphing is the data used as the basis of a graph. To begin with, Paradox (naturally enough) graphs only Numeric data. Chapter 8 referred to a table of sales figures, broken down by salesperson and by month. A portion of the table appears in Figure 12.1. (It includes additional columns for April through June, which are not visible in the figure.)

Figure 12.1

A table from which a graph can be drawn.

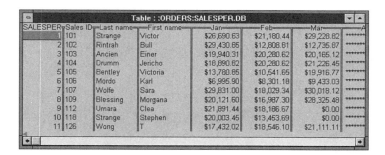

This table happens to be perfect for producing a graph be-cause, by default, Paradox produces a bar graph. Choose Quick Graph by one of the three means suggested, and you'll see the dialog box shown in Figure 12.2. Pull down the table list box to choose a value for the X axis (as you can see, I've chosen Last name). Next, check Y-value and choose for the Y values from the table list box. (In this example, I'll use all six of the month fields.) Finally, choose OK. The resulting graph, using the default graph settings, appears in Figure 12.3.

Compare the graph to the table on which it's based. You'll see that the title of the graph is the same as the name of the table. The labels on the bars are based on the X-axis value chosen, and the order in which the Y-values appear within the bars is the same as the order in the Y-value list box. (You can change the order by using the up arrow and down arrow buttons or by selecting the fields from the list box in a different order.)

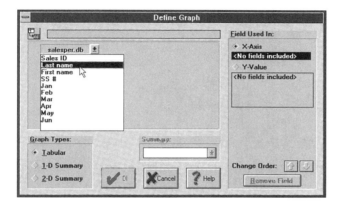

Figure 12.2
The Define Graph dialog box.

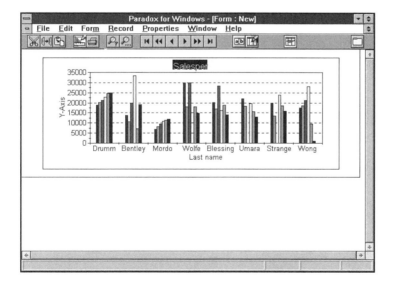

Figure 12.3
A default graph from the SALESPER table.

Notice that the default graph is simply a form with a graph in it. (I've maximized the window so you can see the entire graph.) You can add anything to this window that you would add to a form by choosing Form Design, pressing F8, or clicking the Design button. You can also, as with any other form, open the form as a report and add whatever you feel is appropriate to the report.

Notice also that the title of the graph is highlighted. In a sense, the graph is a field in the form, and the title is the data area. Later in the chapter, we'll make use of that fact to improve this graph.

Graphs from More Complex Data

More often than not, the items you want to graph aren't all neatly arrayed in one table. Depending on what you want to graph, you can either:

- Create a query to put the data in the form you want.

  or

- Create a new form or report, define a data model including all the tables containing relevant data, and use the Graph tool to create a dummy graph which you'll customize.

Since creating a query is simpler, let's look at that first.

Setting Up a Graph Query

Suppose you wanted a six-month comparison of your salespeople, rather than a month-by-month comparison. You could set up the query shown in Figure 12.4, which would produce the accompanying ANSWER table. From there, it's simple to set up the graph in Figure 12.5.

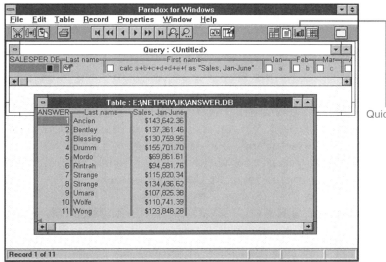

Figure 12.4

A query to group data for graphing.

Quick Graph Icon

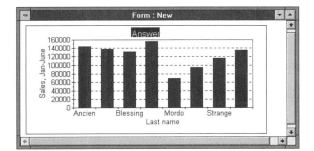

Figure 12.5

A graph from the grouped data.

TIP: If you need to make a graph of summary data (sums, counts, and so on of items listed separately in the source table), first create a query to produce the summary data. Then attach the form containing the graph to the query, rather than to a table.

Data Model

There are actually three points at which you can create a graph: as you already know, you can create a Quick Graph from a table window. You can also create a graph in either a form or a report design window by clicking the Graph tool. This lets you place a "graph object" in your design window by dragging until you have defined its borders. The graph object is simply a dummy graph with no values attached, as shown in Figure 12.6. (This is the same type of object you get to work with when you customize a graph; all graphs take this form in Design mode.)

Figure 12.6
A dummy graph.

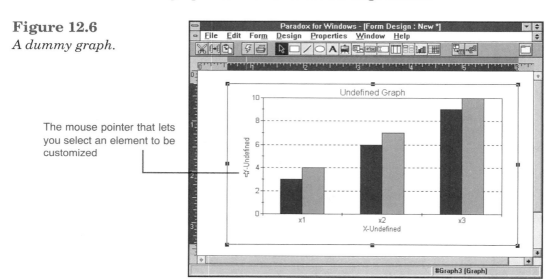

The mouse pointer that lets you select an element to be customized

For example, suppose you wanted to graph the number of orders from each state from the data collected using your order entry application. You'd need a data model containing two tables—CUSTOMER.DB for the State field and ORDERS.DB for the number of orders. Follow these steps:

1. Select File New Form.

2. Set up the data model. Choose the customer.db and orders.db tables, and move them to the center box.

3. Draw the link from orders.db to customer.db.

4. Choose OK.

5. Choose Blank from the Style area of the dialog box.

6. Choose OK.

7. Maximize the design window.

8. Click on the Graph tool and drag the pointer in the design window to create a relatively large area for your graph. You'll see a graph like the one in Figure 12.8.

9. Bring up Object Inspector by the method of your choice.

10. Select Define Graph to enter Define Graph dialog box.

11. In the **Graph Type** area, choose **1**-D Summary. This will make the Summary list box available.

12. For the X-Axis, pull down the customer.db list box and choose State.

13. Click the Y-Value button, pull down the orders.db list box, and choose a field. (Since there is only one record per order in this table, and you want a count, you must choose an item unique to each record; choose Order no.)

14. Pull down the Summary list box, and choose Count. Your screen should now look like Figure 12.7.

15. When you press F8 or click the View Data button, your sales figures should appear in the graph, with appropriate values placed on the X- and Y-axis ticks. Choose OK.

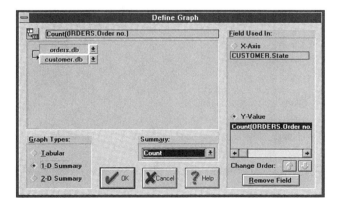

Figure 12.7

Setting up a graph using two tables.

Figure 12.8
A design graph based on two tables.

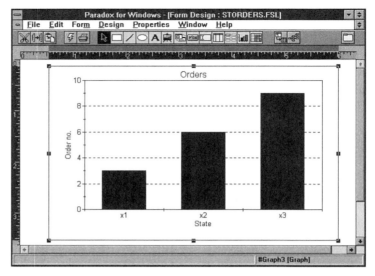

Creating Quick Graphs

1. If necessary, create a query to group and/or summarize the items to be graphed.

2. Select the table containing the items to be graphed.

3. Press Ctrl + F7 or click on the Quick Graph icon on the speedbar or choose Table Quick Graph.

   Paradox displays the Define Graph dialog box.

4. Select the field for the X-axis values from the table's drop-down list of fields.

5. Select the field(s) for the Y-axis values from the table's drop-down list of fields.

6. If the graph is a summary graph, select the type of summary from the Summary list.

7. Choose OK.

Paradox displays a graph having the title of the table, the field name of the X-axis field, and the label Y-axis.

8. Right-click the mouse inside the graph area or choose Properties Current Object or press F6 and select the Graph Type.

9. Add styling as desired by opening the Object Inspector on various parts of the graph.

Customizing Graphs

You customize graphs by inspecting the properties of various elements in them. First you must be in design mode. Next, select the graph. (The outer border represents the page.) When the mouse pointer takes its normal form, you can customize the graph as a whole. When the pointer changes to the form shown in Figure 12.6, you can customize the item being pointed to. You can customize any of these items:

- The X axis
- The Y axis
- The grid (including the background)
- The frame
- The title
- The legend (including whether or not one appears)
- Each of the series displayed

The Main Graph Properties Menu

You view the primary graph menu, shown in Figure 12.9, by clicking the left mouse button when the mouse pointer has its normal form. It is shown with the menu of graph types available.

The commands on the main **Graph** menu have the following effects:

Figure 12.9

The main graph properties menu showing graph types.

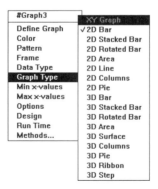

Define Graph brings up the Define Graph dialog box.

Color lets you choose a color for the background of the entire graph frame.

Pattern lets you choose from a palette of patterns, which will be applied to the entire graph frame; a second command lets you choose a color for the pattern.

Frame displays palettes from which you can choose a style and color for the frame surrounding the graph; the palettes are the same as those for frames around fields.

Data Type lets you determine whether your graph should be based on a table, on a one-dimensional summary, or on a two-dimensional summary. You'll learn about one-dimensional summaries shortly; two-dimensional summaries are beyond the scope of this book.

Min x-values lets you select the minimum number of values the graph will display along the X-axis (the default is 8); you can choose from a list of 1 through 8, or choose .. to bring up a dialog box that lets you enter higher numbers.

Max x-values lets you specify the maximum number of values to display along the X-axis; again the default is 8, and the options work the same as for the minimum x-value.

Options determines whether or not certain parts of the graph are displayed. You can check or uncheck Show Title, Show Legend, Show Grid, Show Axes, and Show Labels. By default, a title, a grid, and axes are displayed.

Run Time lets you make a graph invisible by unchecking Visible. You can also uncheck Tab Stop to remove the highlight from the graph title.

The other options are beyond the scope of this book.

In the following example, I'll customize the graph based on the monthly data for each salesperson, and you'll get a look at the subsidiary menus and their uses.

TIP: All the records may not appear in the graph. As you'll remember, the default maximum X-value is 8. There are 11 records in the table. There are two ways to deal with this:

- The easier, obviously, is to change the maximum X-value.

- If you have too many values to fit on the screen, regardless, you can use the Field tool to create a field on the form, outside the graph (in this example, I'd use Last name). You can then scroll through the records in the table by selecting this field and pressing [PgDn]. As you reach records that are not shown in the graph, the graph will scroll to include the latest selected record.

I'll begin by making some global changes. First, I'll select Form Page Layout and change the page size to match that of the screen, as judged by the horizontal and vertical rulers. (For some reason, Paradox's default graph uses only about half the screen's area.)

Next, I'll use the Object Inspector to make the following changes:

1. Put a frame on the graph.

2. Choose Options Show Legend to display a legend for the series.

3. Choose Run Time Tab Stop to remove the highlight from the title.

4. Choose Max x-values and enter a value of 11.

5. Choose the Graph Type menu and change the graph to a 2D Stacked Bar graph.

The result of these changes appears in Figure 12.10.

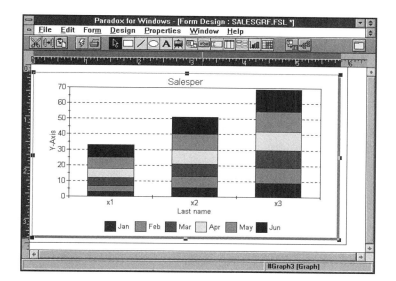

Figure 12.10
A design graph showing global changes.

The Title Object Inspector

Next, I'll customize the title. Right-clicking on the title area displays the menu shown in Figure 12.11. Choosing Title Text lets you type in a new title for your graph. You can, as usual, customize all aspects of the font in which it's displayed. You can also choose a color and pattern for the background behind the title. The Subtitle menu has the same options as the Title menu.

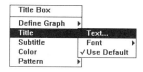

Figure 12.11
The Title Object Inspector.

The Axis Object Inspector

Turn your attention now to the Y-axis. Its Object Inspector appears in Figure 12.12.

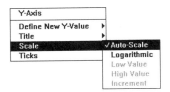

Define New Y-Value brings up a list of the fields in the data model. If you wish, you can change the field on which this value is based from this point, instead of going back to the data model window.

Title lets you change the title, and the way it's displayed. As usual, you can choose the font, color, size, and style of the typeface.

Scale lets you customize the starting and ending points and the interval of the Y-axis scale. To use these features, you must first uncheck Auto-Scale.

Ticks lets you pick a font and numeric format for the values at the Y-axis ticks.

The X-axis Object Inspector also lets you define a new value, change the text and styling of the title, and customize the ticks. The interval of the ticks, however, is fixed. You can choose only the characteristics of the typeface, and whether every tick or only alternate ticks should be labeled. I've entered new titles for both axes, but kept the default values for everything else.

Legend Properties

Click in the legend to display the Legend Object Inspector. As with most other objects, you can select a background color and pattern (and the color of the pattern) for the legend box. Choosing Legend Pos lets you decide whether the legend should be at the bottom of the graph (the default) or at the right.

Grid and Series Properties

Right-clicking in the grid, but away from the graph bars, lets you choose a color, a pattern, and a color for the pattern of the background behind the actual graph.

Right-clicking on any of the series items (including its legend) brings up the menu shown in Figure 12.13. As you can see, at this point you can choose the color and pattern for the series. You can also remove the value from the graph (bypassing the Define Graph dialog box) or assign the series to a different field.

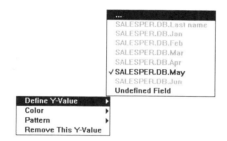

Figure 12.13
The Series properties menu.

I've added a colored pattern to each of the series and another to the grid. Figure 12.14 shows the data displayed in the graph. As you can see, it's still not quite right. Bars appear for all the sales employees, but only half of them are labeled, so we can't see who half of the bars belong to. To remedy this situation, I could, as mentioned, put a Last name field outside the graph, and reduce the maximum x-values to 8 again.

CAUTION

You may think that you could display all the values and all the X-axis titles by reopening the form as a report. But the same graph specification will result in a series of separate graphs, one for each value on the X-axis (in this case, one for each employee).

Figure 12.14
*A fully styled
graph.*

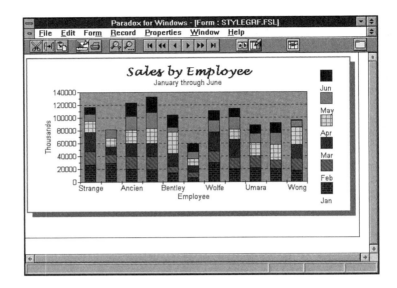

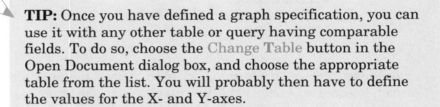

TIP: Once you have defined a graph specification, you can use it with any other table or query having comparable fields. To do so, choose the Change Table button in the Open Document dialog box, and choose the appropriate table from the list. You will probably then have to define the values for the X- and Y-axes.

Creating Crosstabs

Paradox includes one more facility for viewing your data: *crosstabs*. Sometimes you may want to see one item classified in terms of another just to get a different view of your data. You also need to have your data in that format in order to create a series graph, if it isn't already in that format (as it was in the SALESPER table).

This facility works tolerably well if you want a count of items in a single field.

Crosstabs are available only in forms, not in reports. Here's an example of a simple crosstab:

1. Choose File New Form.

2. Select the ORDERS.DB table for the data model, and choose OK.

3. In the Style area of the Design Layout dialog box, choose Blank. Choose OK.

4. Maximize the design window. Choose the Crosstab tool and drag to create a box somewhat like the one in Figure 12.15.

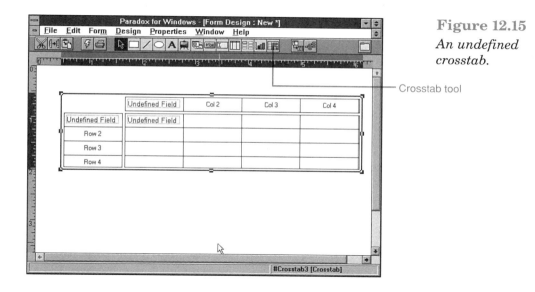

Figure 12.15
An undefined crosstab.

5. Right-click somewhere in the box, and choose Define Crosstab from the Object Inspector. Choose the three dots to get to the Define Crosstab dialog box, which appears filled out in Figure 12.16.

6. Pull down the orders.db list box, and select Ship via for the Column definition.

7. Choose Summaries. From the orders.db list box, select a field (again, since we're getting a count, use one that won't recur, such as Order no).

8. Choose Summary. From the drop-down list, select Count.

9. Choose OK.

10. Select the field labeled Count(ORDE. It's in the first column of the first row, not the row or column headers. Open the Object Inspector and choose Format Number Format Integer.

11. Click the View Data button, or press F8. You should now see how many of your customers used each shipping method, as shown in Figure 12.17.

If you go back into design mode, you can, as usual, right-click anywhere to style anything. You can also readjust the size of the box so that it looks more reasonable.

Figure 12.16

The Define Crosstab dialog box.

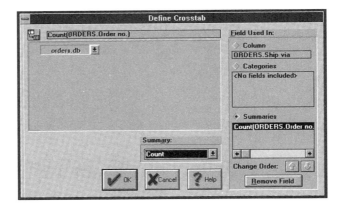

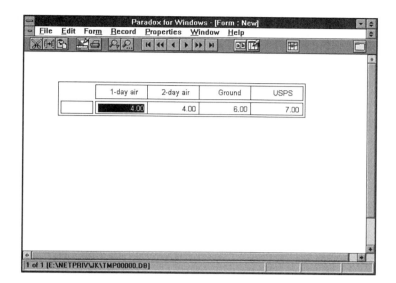

Figure 12.17
*A completed
crosstab.*

A

Installing Paradox on Your Computer

As mentioned in Chapter 1, you must have a hard disk in order to use Paradox for Windows. I'll assume that you do and that your computer is not connected to a network. (Installation procedures are different if you will be using Paradox on a network.)

Before you install Paradox, make a backup copy of all the floppy disks on the size disks appropriate for your computer. First make sure you have the same number of blank floppy disks (or floppy disks with data that you no longer need) as the floppy disks you will copy. Go to the DOS prompt (`C:>`) and type `DISKCOPY A: A:`.

NOTE: If you received the wrong kind of disks for your computer, you'll find a coupon allowing you to exchange them for the right kind. You can also purchase a second set of disks of a different type for a nominal fee.

You will then see a message telling you to place the source floppy disk into drive A and to press a key. Place one of the Paradox floppy disks into drive A. You will be told to swap the source (that is, the Paradox floppy disk) and the target (the blank or reused) floppy disk several times until the copy is complete. You will then be asked if you wish to copy another. Press Y and press ↵Enter, until you have copied all the floppy disks.

To begin installing Paradox for Windows, you must first load Windows. Next, insert Disk 1 into one of your floppy disk drives. Paradox can be installed equally well from either drive A or drive B.

When the floppy disk is in your selected drive, choose File Run from the Program Manager's menu. In the text box, enter a:install or b:install, depending on the floppy disk drive you're using. The Paradox for Windows Installation menu appears, as shown in Figure A.1. You must enter your name, company name, and the serial number from Disk 1 (which you'll have to take out of the drive), and press Tab↹ after each.

Figure A.1

*The Paradox
Installation menu.*

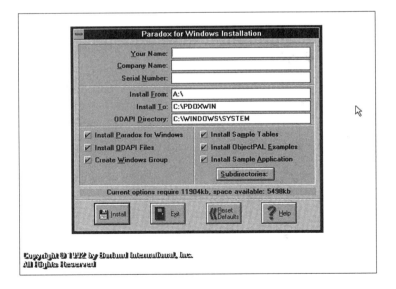

If you wish to have Paradox for Windows installed in a directory other than C:\PDOXWIN, edit the Install **T**o text box so that it shows the name of your desired directory. If your Windows directory is on a drive other than C, move to the ODAPI **D**irectory text box, press Home, press Del, and enter the correct drive letter.

You'll notice groups of check boxes on the bottom half of the menu. Leave the ones on the left checked. These tell the installation program to install Paradox for Windows, to install some essential files that Paradox requires, and to create a group file in the Program Manager containing Paradox itself, the Table Repair Utility, and the Configuration Utility, along with some text files containing the latest information on these items. You won't be able to run Paradox from Windows easily if you don't have this group, although you can create it yourself, or use the File Run command if you prefer.

The check boxes on the right side of the screen install some sample tables and two sample applications—one to help you learn Paradox for Windows interactively and the other to help you learn to program in ObjectPAL. If you need to conserve disk space or don't plan to use these files, uncheck these boxes. If you wish to install them, you can choose the Subdirectories button to edit the names of the subdirectories in which they will be placed. (By default they will be subdirectories of the directory in which you install Paradox for Windows itself.) When you finish making your selections, choose Install. You'll see the screen shown in Figure A.2. Periodically, road signs will appear giving you information about Paradox's features. You'll also see dialog boxes instructing you to place a different disk in the drive and select OK. Follow the instructions.

When the installation is complete, you'll see a message telling you so. Choose OK. The program will have installed all the elements of Paradox you selected, in the specified directories, and created two empty directories below Paradox's main directory: PRIVATE and WORKING.

The box that tells you that the work is done also says that if you want several applications to read from the same Paradox tables, you must install SHARE, a program that's part of DOS. To do that, type

```
C:\DOS\SHARE /F:4096 /L:400
```

at a DOS prompt before you load Windows. If you always use Windows, you should place this line in your AUTOEXEC.BAT file.

Figure A.2
Installing Paradox for Windows.

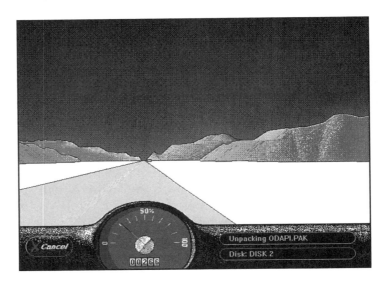

CAUTION

Do not load SHARE from a DOS window inside of Windows.

Index

To Order Companion Disk

The companion disk contains all the files developed in *The First Book of Paradox for Windows*. The 5¼" disk is formatted to 360K and the 3½" disk is formatted to 720K.

The disk may be purchased with cash, check, or money order. Purchase price includes shipping and handling. All orders will be shipped by first class mail. Make checks and money orders payable to Kamin Consulting Services. (No phone orders, please.)

Send this form with payment in U.S. funds to:

Kamin Consulting Services
445 Second St., Suite 212
Lake Oswego, OR 97034

Alpha Books assumes no liability with respect to the use or accuracy of the information contained on these disks.

— —

Disk Order Form

Kamin, *The First Book of Paradox for Windows*, #27402-7

(Please print)

Name_____

Company _____

Address_____

City_____State_____ZIP _____

County_____Phone (   ) _____

Place of Book Purchase_____

5¼"
Quantity_____ @ $20 U.S.   Total: $ _____

3½"
Quantity_____ @ $21 U.S.   Total: $ _____

Method of Payment
Check # _____ Money Order # _____

All orders will be shipped U.S. Postal Service First Class.
Please allow six weeks for delivery.